Death

at

The Davison Home

Texas City's Most
Infamous Murder

By: Matthew Daniels

Table of Contents

Introduction

On September 19, 1970, a 75-year-old woman was brutally raped and murdered inside of her own home. This woman was Mrs. Ida C. Davison, and the home she was murdered inside of was The Davison Home. The Davison family are pioneers in Texas City, Tx., and their family quite literally helped to found our wonderful city.

Although The Davison Home is one of the most well-known structures in all of Texas City, Tx., not many people know about the brutal murder that took place there so many decades ago. Even those who have a cursory knowledge of the murder have no clue about the horrific details I am about to reveal in this book.

I was able to uncover the actual murder file associated with this case and a plethora of newspaper articles, court documents, census records, and pictures that tell this story like no one has ever told it before in Texas City history. At the end of this book, I will include the actual murder file itself for your perusal.

Buckle up, dear reader, this True Crime story will be one like you have never heard before.

Chapter 1

The 911 Call That Started It All

"911. What's your emergency?" The dispatcher officer for the Texas City Police Department answered the call in his usual fashion.

"Oh my God! Oh my God! Oh my God!" A male voice cried out in panic on the other end of the line. "Somebody's been hurt badly. I need an ambulance and the police to come quick. Please!"

"Ok sir." The dispatcher replied, sitting upright in his seat. "I need you to try to remain calm. Where are you?"

"Uuummm, I'm at my church, officer." The caller answered, peeking out the back door of the building. "But they need you to send the ambulance to 109 3rd Avenue North. Over here at The Davison Home. They're out there screaming bloody murder, sir. Something horrible has happened from the looks of it. You all need to hurry up."

"Don't worry." The dispatcher said. "I'm going to send an officer and an ambulance right away. Can you tell me who it is that's been hurt?"

The officer immediately began writing down the address the caller had given him and all other details he was receiving from the call. When he heard that the call for assistance was at The Davison Home, his mind began racing.

What could possibly be going on at The Davison Home, he wondered?

"Uuuhhh. I don't know, sir." The caller said, rubbing his head. "A lady, I believe. They say she's hurt badly, sir. Please, just send help immediately."

"Ok sir. I'm sending units over now. Just hang tight. Stay on the phone with me until they arrive."

Officer Schoolcraft instantly sprang into action. He called for any unit in the area of the 911 call to head over there immediately, and he also contacted Crowder Ambulance Services. Within seconds of the phone call, the police were hurriedly responding to an unknown situation. They had no clue at the time, but the 911 call they were responding to about a lady hurt badly at The Davison Home would soon go down in history as Texas City's most infamous murder.

No 102

3 88

Police Department

COMPLAINT NO. 11388   DATE 9-19-70   TIME 0942

NAME (Rev.) didn't understand last name   PHONE

ADDRESS 3rd Ave. & 1st N

REPORTS Women hurt badly need a amb.

Crowder notified

DISP. Schoolcraft

OFFICER ASSIGNED 737 Henry 759 Oliver

OFFICER REPORT

DATE 9-15-70   OFFICER

Murder File: Actual 911 Call Report

9

Chapter 2

Texas City Woman, 75, Murdered

Galveston Daily News September 20, 1970

Officer Schoolcraft, the dispatch officer who took the 911 call that day, did not realize at the time that that one 911 call would become etched upon the pages of Texas City history forever. What occurred on Saturday morning, September 19, 1970, set off a chain of events that would become burned into the psyche of Texas City Citians for several decades to come, and it would become known as Texas City's most infamous murder. That 911 call led to a headline being printed in The Galveston Daily News the next day that was explosive, horrific, terrifying, and sorrowful.

Texas City Woman, 75, Murdered!

Phone lines lit up in the wake of this tragic event. The traditional channels through which the sorted details of local gossip were disseminated to a public eagerly anticipating salacious morsels of little-known knowledge all put an immediate halt to the mundane tales of lewd and lascivious gossip, and the story on everyone's lips was the tale of the death at The Davison Home. Both men and women, rich and poor, members of high society and members of the city's lower class, all had an opinion on the matter. Indeed, a small town like Texas City, where everyone knew everyone, a murder of a member of the Davison family no doubt sparked countless conspiracy theories and controversies.

Amidst the uncertainty that followed that newspaper headline, there were even suspicions that a serial killer might be on the loose in Texas City. Some people hypothesized that there was a sick and twisted killer running amok, stalking the most vulnerable in their community and savagely attacking them in the sanctity of their own homes. After all, what kind of person would attack and kill a 75-year-old woman in her own home? What kind of person would target a grandmother, a faithful Christian, and a woman who lived her life in the service of others? Of course, that person was the lowest of the low. The proverbial scum of the earth. The bottom of the barrel of humanity. An individual so heartless, inhumane, and evil, that no one was safe while they were allowed to roam the streets of Texas City.

Unbeknownst to the general public, however, on Sunday morning when that headline was delivered to the homes of tens of thousands of residents in Galveston County, the Texas City Police Department already had a suspect in custody, and the process of gathering evidence and piecing together the particulars of the crime were already underway. It is true that the court system of the United States has the difficult task of proving guilt and sentencing criminals to prison, but it is the job of the police to capture these criminals and compile the evidence that the prosecutors will eventually use against them in court. If the police arrest the wrong suspect, or if the police do not collect the evidence in the proper manner, it is virtually impossible for the courts to condemn the guilty.

Unfortunately for the suspect, but fortunately for the victim and the community, the high-profile nature of the woman who was murdered ensured that all necessary steps were taken to arrest the correct person and see that justice was served. It was bad enough that the victim was a 75-year-old woman, but the identity of the woman herself caused more shockwaves than simply the crime itself. As shameful as it might be, murder is not as uncommon as we would hope. Young and old alike regularly fall victim to the sick and twisted blood-lust fantasies of the absolute worst in our societies. It is not every day, however, that the person who is murdered is well known, highly respected, and a member of the most famous family in all of Texas City.

When the public read the headlines that Sunday morning, the name of the deceased hit everyone directly in their chest as if they had just been run over by an 18-wheeler going 65 mph down I-45.

Mrs. Ida C. Davison.

Mrs. Ida Davison was the loving wife of Mr. Donald (Don) C. Davison. **(See Photo 1A at the end of this chapter.)** Mr. Don C. Davison was the son of Frank and Florence Davison. **(See Photo 2A at the end of this chapter.)** Frank Davison is considered by many to be the main founding father of Texas City, and it was him and his wife who began construction on The Davison Home in 1895. The history of The Davison Home and the Davison family, however, dates back to 1893 when Frank Davison, accompanied by his wife Florence, arrived at Shoal Point, a sleepy village that later developed into the community of Texas City. Which is why I say that Frank Davison founded Texas City, because when he migrated here from Michigan, the city now known as Texas City was called Shoal Point.

Frank Davison came to the area as resident manager of the Texas City Improvement Company, which had just purchased the town of Shoal Point and renamed it Texas City. Development of the community was just beginning, and the Davison couple made many investments to ensure that their community had certain business services.

Such services initiated by Frank Davison included the community's first general store, the first real estate company, a lumber yard, a flour mill, and a hotel. The pioneer resident of Texas City also served as the first postmaster from 1893 to 1897, as one of the first two city commissioners, as a director of the first bank, and as a member of the school board. In fact, the list of firsts for the Davison's goes even further than that. The very first baby born in the newly named City of Texas City was born inside of The Davison Home.

In 1896, two years before the Improvement Company's bankruptcy, Mrs. Davison sold her stock in the company with the thought of beginning construction of a home. Two years were required to build the home, with materials being shipped by boat from Louisiana.

Great care was taken to ensure a sturdy, permanent home, indicating the faith the Davison's had in the budding young town. The home contained the first telephone in the city and was the site of the organization of the Garden Club and the Study Club. Over the years, the city hosted Easter Egg Hunts at The Davison Home, and it was as if everyone in the city was somehow connected to both the family and the Victorian style home. **(See Photo 3A, 4A, and 5A at the end of this chapter.)**

So, when the Texas City Citizens, and the Texas City Police Department came to the realization that the 911 call was made in reference to the trailblazing Davison family, literally all hands were on deck to solve this crime and to solve this crime as quickly as possible. It was as if the city itself was attacked. Not to mention all of the good Mrs. Ida Davison did in her community. Even when people find justification for certain murders by pointing out the dangerous lifestyle of the individual killed, no one could comprehend any logical reason that would cause a person to murder Mrs. Ida Davison in cold blood.

According to the official records, when the 911 call was made to the Texas City Police Department, Officer Schoolcraft was working dispatch. The call came through early that Saturday morning, at 9:42 a.m., on September 19, 1970. The caller was a man named Rev. Jesse Ruefenacht who presided over the 2nd Ave Church of God, located directly behind The Davison Home. The church building stood to the south of the crime scene, and it is actually still standing at the time of the writing of this work. **(See Photo 6A at the end of this chapter.)** Rev. Ruefenacht explained to the police that he was sitting inside the church building with his wife, Mrs. Ruefenacht, and a pastor named Rev. George Hawkins. Rev Hawkins was staying with them at the time, and he was present when they heard a male and female voice calling for help outside.

Upon hearing the calls for help, these 3 individuals stepped outside of the church and looked across the alley behind them towards The Davison Home. What they saw rocked them all to their very core. Just a few feet away, frantically calling for someone to call an ambulance and the police, the trio saw a white male and white female standing in the back yard of The Davison Home. The two individuals were yelling that their mother had been hurt, there was blood everywhere, and the sheer horror that they were experiencing was clearly etched deeply upon both of their faces.

The woman and man who were calling out for help turned out to be none other than Mr. and Mrs. E.J. Opersteny. Mrs. Opersteny, born Mary Ella Davison, was the daughter of Mrs. Ida Davison, and we can only imagine how the gruesome scene affected her mentally. The trauma of it can only be guessed at, but her actions give us a glimpse into her immediate thoughts after finding the woman who gave birth to her and raised her in such a compromised position. The fact that she and her husband immediately rushed outside and begged for the neighbors to call the police, speaks volumes. It tells us that the scene they encountered was so horrific and terrifying, that in addition to sensing fear for her mother's condition, she also felt an extreme sense of fear for herself and her husband.

After all, at that point, they had no way of knowing if the culprit was still inside of the home somewhere hiding out waiting for more victims. There was a fully operational telephone inside of The Davison Home, but the couple chose not to use it. Instead, they yelled until they got the attention of the neighbors and asked them to call the police for them.

As you can see from the photos I've included at the end of this chapter, The Davison Home is not a small one-room home. On the contrary. At the time of this event, it was possibly the largest home in all of Texas City. In fact, it is still one of the largest homes in Texas City over 100 years after it was built. The house itself is a three-story home built in a style reminiscent of the Victorian Era architecture, and it can easily be described as a mansion. So, subsequently, there were plenty of places for a criminal to hide on the inside. Luckily, it did not take long for the police to arrive on the scene.

The first two officers to arrive on the scene were Texas City Police Officers Richard Henry and Deril Oliver. Upon reaching the residence, the pair was directed to the back of the house by several concerned neighbors who had flooded out into the street because of the commotion. When the pair reached the back of the house they were met by, and spoke with, Mr. and Mrs. Opersteny.

After being told who the victim was, and where the victim's body was located inside of the home, the two officers proceeded to enter the residence. They approached cautiously from the south, which was the back of the home, with their guns drawn. All of their training instantly kicked in and they instinctively knew that they needed to be prepared for any eventuality. They slowly but purposefully walked towards the back door which sat on the southeast corner of the residence. This door led directly into the kitchen where the victim was reported to be.

Officer Henry stated that upon entering the kitchen and scanning the scene, he observed the body of an elderly white female lying on the floor with her head towards the back door he was entering through. The body was clad in a white slip under a pink and white housecoat. He observed that both the slip and the housecoat the victim was wearing were pushed up above the waist exposing the lower half of her body. His mouth dropped when he saw that her nether regions were completely nude and exposed. The minds of the officers began to race. Both of them had grandmothers which they loved dearly. The sight of an elderly woman in such a compromised position caused a lump to form in their throats.

"What the hell happened here?" They both thought, as their brains struggled to process the violence before them.

The body itself was resting on its back with the arms at the sides, and the legs were spread apart. The officers noticed a wound on the right side of her forehead and her head was surrounded by a large amount of blood. There was a growing pool of blood on the floor and multiple blood splatters on the wall next to the head. There was also blood oozing out the mouth of the victim, and their blood visible at the vaginal area. The blood smeared around the vaginal area told a particularly gruesome tale indeed. It indicated that in addition to being ambushed inside the sanctity of her own home and brutally assaulted, the 75-year-old Mrs. Ida Davison, was also mercilessly raped by the perpetrator of this crime.

Under closer examination of the body, the police officers on the scene noticed that Mrs. Davison was injured, but not dead. She was unconscious; however, breathing could be detected. Perhaps she could be saved. The officers knew that there was an ambulance on the way, so they did the best they could to keep Mrs. Davison breathing while they waited on emergency services. They also split up and did a quick search of the rest of the house; however, the culprit was not found inside. The officers then called Police Chief Rankin DeWalt and alerted him to the situation at the crime scene. **(See Photo 7A at the end of this chapter.)**

After securing the location and confirming that the culprit was no longer on the premises, the two officers tended to Mrs. Ida Davison until emergency services arrived and rushed her off to get lifesaving treatment. Next, they switched into investigative mode and proceeded to take down a statement from Mr. and Mrs. Opersteny so that they could try and ascertain exactly what took place. Mrs. Opersteny stated that at approximately 9:00 a.m. that Saturday morning she attempted to call her mother who lived at the residence with her husband.

Mrs. Opersteny went on to say that when she called, her mother never picked up the phone. That was weird because she spoke with her mother regularly, and every time she called, her mother would always answer the phone on the first or second ring. The mother and daughter duo had a routine. Mrs. Opersteny would often call her mother several times per day in order to check on her. For one, the two of them had a very close relationship since Mrs. Opersteny was a child. Also, Mrs. Ida Davison was 75 years old, and her husband, who was just as elderly as she was, still went to work almost every single day around 7:45 a.m. Mrs. Davison was left home alone a lot to tend to her chores around the house and to plan events and meetings for groups such as The Garden Club which she was once the president of. Mrs. Opersteny felt that it was her responsibility to regularly check in with her elderly mother.

After not receiving an answer to her first phone call, Mrs. Opersteny called back several times thinking that perhaps her mother was away from the phone in the bathroom or something. Or maybe she was dealing with the family dog that the Davison's owned. At first, Mrs. Opersteny considered several logical explanations for the silence. However, at approximately 9:30 a.m. she began to worry. Because of this, she convinced her husband, Mr. E.J. Opersteny, to drive her up the street to her mother's home so that she could check on her. After all, Mr. and Mrs. Opersteny lived at 416 10th Ave N at the time, and that was only around 3-5 minutes away from The Davison Home. It would be nothing to swing by real quick and perform a wellness check.

When Mr. and Mrs. Opersteny arrived at The Davison Home, they parked in the back of the home and noticed that the screen door was closed but the inner wooden door was wide open. That was not weird in and of itself, seeing as how Mrs. Davison would often open the front and back door to allow the air from outside to flow freely through her home to cool it off.

Upon reaching the back door, the couple peered in through the screen door. When they did, they were totally unprepared for the sight that they encountered. What they saw was the body of the elderly Mrs. Ida Davison lying on the kitchen floor in a pool of what appeared to be her own blood. Seeing this, both Mr. and Mrs. Opersteny panicked and began yelling for someone to call the police and an ambulance. As much as she wanted her instincts to be wrong, Mrs. Opersteny had her worst fears confirmed. There was indeed a sinister reason why her mother had not answered her many phone calls.

Multiple neighbors heard their pleas for help and came outside to investigate, but the one that actually made the 911 call was Rev. Ruefenacht. Officer Oliver and Officer Henry then spoke with Rev. Ruefenacht, his wife, and Rev. George Hawkins. All 3 of them told the same story. They claimed that they were all inside the church prior to making to the 911 call when they heard someone screaming outside. Curious, they went outside to investigate the source of the cries for help. Upon learning that a lady was inside of The Davison Home badly hurt, Rev. Ruefenacht called the police and requested assistance.

Rev. Ruefenacht and his wife lived in Texas City for years, however, I do not know with 100% certainty where Rev. George Hawkins was from. According to the official statement he gave to the police, he owned a P.O box that had an address of P.O. Box 1203, Rockport. So, one could assume he was from Rockport, Tx, some 182 miles away from Texas City, Tx. The fact that he gave the police a P.O. Box instead of a physical address, coupled with the fact that he was living with the Ruefenacht's at the time of the 911 call, leads me to believe he had no place of his own to call home.

Although all 3 people corroborated each other's story, the police made a mental note that Rev. Hawkins was an outsider to the Texas City community. In the early stages of any police investigation everyone is a suspect. Family, friends, and even witnesses. Police training teaches them to consider everyone a suspect and then eliminate potential suspects as they gather more and more evidence. The fact that Rev. Hawkins was a pastor meant close to nothing. Men of the cloth committed crimes just like gangbangers and thugs committed them.

Within minutes of the police arriving, Crowder Ambulance Services arrived and swiftly transported the victim to Galveston Memorial Hospital where lifesaving methods were initiated. Shortly after that, Police Chief Rankin DeWalt arrived at the crime scene with Texas City's first ever Hispanic officer, Lt. Saragoza. **(See Photo 8A at the end of this chapter.)**

At first glance, when someone hears that the Chief of Police arrived at the scene of a crime within minutes of it being reported, it might sound a tad bit out of place or unbelievable. I mean, the chief doesn't respond to every single 911 call. Why would he respond to this one? But, when we consider what I just explained about the prominence of the Davison family, it makes perfect sense why the Chief of Police would show up to take a hands-on approach to solving this particular case.

Not to mention, in a sense, Police Chief Rankin DeWalt was actually an underling of Mr. Don C. Davison, the husband of the victim. Mr. Don. C. Davison was the Master Mason of the Texas City Masonic Lodge #1118 in 1921. In 1967, he was also presented with a 50-year Grand Lodge service award for being the first member to be raised to Master Mason in the Texas City Lodge.

TC Lodge To Observe It's 50th Anniversary

TEXAS CITY—The observance of the 50th anniversary of Texas City Lodge 1118 AF&AM Friday night will be a three-fold affair.

A 50-year Grand Lodge service award will be presented to the first member to be raised to Master Mason in the Texas City Lodge, along with retiring the original charter and honoring all past masters.

Don. C. Davison will be presented the 50-year award by J. W. Chandler of Houston, deputy grand master of the Grand Lodge of Texas.

Chandler will also present L. R. Haire, worshipful master of the Texas City Lodge, with a copy of the original charter so that the original may be preserved.

Only on 50th and 100th anniversaries or following destruction by some disaster does a lodge receive a copy of its original charter.

Past masters of the Texas City Lodge will be guests at a dinner to be served at 6:30 p.m. preceding the ceremonies in the lodge at 7:30 Friday.

The Texas City Lodge was chartered Dec. 16, 1916 and "set to work" Dec. 11, 1916, by Grand Master Frank C. Jones.

Galveston Daily News March 12, 1967

TC Lodge To Observe It's 50th Anniversary

TEXAS CITY – The observance of the 50th anniversary of Texas City Lodge 1118 AF & AM Friday night will be a three-fold affair.

A 50-year Grand Lodge service award will be presented to the first member to be raised to Master Mason in the Texas City Lodge, along with retiring the original charter and honoring all past masters.

Don. C. Davison will be presented the 50-year award by J.W. Chandler of Houston, deputy grand master of the Grand Lodge of Texas.

23

Now I am not sure if Mr. Don Davison was actually the first member in Texas City to be raised to the status of Master Mason, or if he was simply the oldest living previous Master Mason alive at the time that could accept the award, but there can be no doubt that he held a position of high importance and significance within the Texas City Lodge. This is evident by the fact that the award was presented to him on behalf of the entire lodge itself.

This status within the lodge granted Mr. Davison a position of authority and notoriety over Chief DeWalt that superseded what normal citizens understand and live by. Especially since Police Chief DeWalt was a faithful member of the exact same lodge that Mr. Davison was once a leader of.

Rankin DeWalt

TEXAS CITY — Rankin L. DeWalt, 75, a resident of Texas City for many years passed away on Thursday, August 29, 1991 at Danforth Hospital in Texas City. Services will be held at 10:00 a.m. Saturday, August 31, 1991, at the First Baptist Church of Texas City with the Reverend Ron Dixon officiating. Burial will follow at Chalk Cemetery near Trinity, Texas, with Masonic graveside services conducted by Texas City Lodge 1118 AF & AM at 4:00 p.m. Saturday.

Mr DeWalt served as Chief of Police in Texas City for over twenty-three years retiring in 1979. He was a graduate of the F.B.I. National Academy. He was a member of the First Baptist Church of Texas City. Mr. DeWalt was a member of the Masonic Lodge 1118 AF & AM of Texas City, a member of the Scottish Rite and the El Mina Shrine Temple.

Upon his retirement, The Texas Senate and House of Representatives passed a Resolution honoring him for his many years of service to the Law Enforcement profession.

He was a veteran of World War II and served in the European Theatre. As a first Lieutenant in the Military Police Corp., he was awarded the Bronze Star Medal for Meritorious Service in crossing the Rhine River in Germany.

He was awarded a lifetime membership in the National Congress of Parent Teachers Association and a lifetime member of the International Association of Chiefs of Police. He was a member of the American Legion and Veterans of Foreign Wars. He was selected by the Junior Chamber of Commerce

Galveston Daily News August 31, 1991

25

Rankin DeWalt

Burial will follow at Chalk Cemetery near Trinity, Texas, with Masonic gravesite services conducted by Texas City Lodge 1118 AF & AM at 4:00 p.m. Saturday.

Mr. DeWalt served as Chief of Police in Texas City for over twenty-three years retiring in 1979. He was a graduate of the F.B.I. National Academy. He was a member of the First Baptist Church of Texas City. Mr. DeWalt was a member of the Masonic Lodge 1118 AF & AM of Texas City, a member of the Scottish Rite and the El Mina Shrine Temple.

Once Chief DeWalt received the call that the wife of someone who outranked him within his Masonic Lodge was assaulted, he not only reacted to the crime as the head of the police department, but he also responded to the call as a Masonic Brother seeking retribution and justice for a past Master Mason of his own lodge. It is my belief that it is this masonic connection between Don Davison and Rankin DeWalt that caused Chief DeWalt to drive out to the actual crime scene personally, and it was this connection that caused him to mobilize the entirety of the Texas City Police Department to capture the suspect and solve the crime.

Photo 1A

Mr. Don C. Davison And Mrs. Ida C. Davison (Circa 1944)

Photo 2A

Mr. Frank Davison And Mrs. Florence Davison With Their Family In Front Of The Davison Home

Photo 3A

The Davison Home (Front View Facing North)

Photo 4A

The Davison Home (Back View Facing South)

Photo 5A

Easter Egg Hunt In The Front Yard Of The Davison Home (Circe 1913)

Photo 6A

The Davison Home

2nd Ave Church Of God. The Davison Home Can Be Seen In The Background

Photo 7A

**Police Chief Rankin L. DeWalt (Left) Stands In The Snow
With A Texas City Cop**

Photo 8A

Lt. Saragoza

Chapter 3

The History Of Mrs. Ida Davison And The Davison Family

Funerals

MONDAY

MRS. DON C. (IDA) DAVISON, 75, of 109 3rd Ave. North, Texas City; funeral services 4:30 p.m. Monday at the First United Methodist Church in Texas City, the Rev. Edwin Summers officiating; burial in La Marque Cemetery under the direction of Emken Linton Funeral Home.

Galveston Daily News September 21, 1970

Funerals

Monday

Mrs. Don C. (Ida) Davison, 75, of 109 3rd Ave. North, Texas City; funeral services 4:30 p.m. Monday at the First United Methodist Church in Texas City, the Rev. Edwin Summers officiating; burial in La Marque Cemetery under the direction of Emken Linton Funeral Home.

When the emergency personnel sped away from the scene of the crime, Mrs. Ida Davison was barely clinging on to life in the back. She was still unconscious, and she was unresponsive, but she was still breathing. Even though she had lost a lot of blood and had suffered a violent attack, that fact alone gave everyone some type of hope.

"Just hang on Mrs. Davison." The first responder called out as he held onto Ida's limp hand. "Keep fighting. We're going to save you. I promise. Just don't... stop... fighting."

The ambulance driver glanced over his shoulder as his colleague continued to encourage their passenger. He knew deep down that her chances of survival were slim. He had seen enough crime scenes to deduce that. Still, he also knew that hope was a powerful medicine. Sometimes an individual could be pulled back from the brink of certain death with sheer willpower alone. Neither of them knew for sure if Mrs. Davison could actually hear the first responder's words of encouragement, but they knew it couldn't hurt to try and reach her.

Unfortunately, though, everyone involved in the crime up until that point had no way of knowing for sure how things would turn out. Not the family, not the police, not the emergency responders, not the neighbors, and not the doctors who were notified that an elderly woman who had been badly hurt was in route to the hospital. You and I, on the other hand, have the benefit of hindsight. We know that no matter what anyone will do that day, the Texas City community will lose a beautiful soul.

In order to better understand how Mrs. Davison died, and why her death had such a profound impact upon the community, we first must understand how she lived. After all, it would surely be an injustice to sum up one's life by the manner of their death. Indeed, we are all so much more than that. And Mrs. Ida Davison, also, was so much more than that. So, who exactly was Mrs. Ida C. Davison?

Mrs. Ida was born around 130 years ago on September 30, 1894. As if it was some type of mystical omen to her future faithful service as a member of the First United Methodist Church, the day of her birth was a Sunday. The same day of the week that billions of Christians around the world believe that Jesus Christ triumphantly defeated death and rose from the dead. Her parents were named Mr. W.E. Woodruff and Mrs. Ella F. (Thompson) Woodruff. Her birthname was Ida Candace Woodruff and she was born in Houston, Tx.

Today, Houston, Tx is one of the largest cities in Texas with a population of around 2.5 million people, but back in the late 1800's when Ida was born, the population was only around 28,000. This means that the Houston she grew up in was much different from the Houston that exists today. Her parents were devoted loving parents, and her childhood was as good as one might expect.

Although she was born in Houston, neither of her parents were even native to the state of Texas. Her father was born in Alabama, and her mother was born in Georgia. It is likely that the two of them moved to Houston, Tx in order to find more opportunities to create a better life for themselves, and in the process, they met each other and found love. Mr.

W.E. Woodruff was also a 32nd degree Mason and a member of the Scottish Rite. Much like Chief Rankin DeWalt, Mr. Don C. Davison, and Texas City pioneer Mr. Frank Davison.

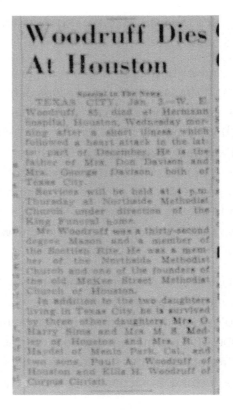

Galveston Daily News January 4, 1951

He is the father of Mrs. Don Davison and Mrs. George Davison, both of Texas City.

Mr. Woodruff was a thirty-second degree Mason and a member of the Scottish Rite.

34

There is no direct evidence to support this hypothesis, however, I believe that Mr. Woodruff met Mr. Frank Davison by moving through Masonic circles, and the two of them became brothers and friends. I say this because two of Mr. Woodruff's daughters married two of Mr. Frank Davison's sons. As we have already established, Ida Woodruff married Donald C. Davion and became Mrs. Ida Davison, but Ida had a sister that married one of the Davison boys as well. Her sister married Mr. George Orrie Davison, and the couple lived in Texas City at the time of Mr. Woodruff's passing.

Why would two sisters from Houston marry two brothers from Texas City if the two families were not close? And as it stands, the only connection I have uncovered so far is the Masonic connection between the fathers of both sets of siblings. Whatever the connection between the two families truly was, we know that on October 13, 1919, Ida Woodruff married Don Davison and officially became Mrs. Ida C. Davison. She was 25 years old at the time and had her whole life ahead of her. **(See Photo 1A and 2A at the end of this chapter.)**

For Ida, Don was her knight in shining armor. He was the love of her life. Her soulmate. The man she dreamed about for countless hours as a child. When he held her in her arms and described the type of life they would one day have together, Ida would just melt. His passionate gaze, warm embrace, and handsome smile had the uncanny ability to make all of her insecurities and fears fade away. He was everything she ever wanted in a husband, and as far as her friends were concerned, Ida had won the proverbial love lottery. Not only was he sweet, kind, and gentle, but he was also a man of vision, ambition, and drive.

Not to mention he came from a family of wealth, prestige, and impeccable pedigree. Don Davison was born in Michigan, and his father Frank was born in Michigan also. His grandfather, on the other hand, was from Ogden, New York, and his grandmother was from Stockton, England. Don's great grandfather, Col. Davison took an active part in the American Revolutionary War, and the family has been identified with the history of the United States since the early colonial days, back when America did not yet exist. There were only the 13 colonies.

Immediately after their marriage in 1919, Ida moved to Texas City, Tx. and moved in with her new husband. The newlyweds were living at 109 3rd Ave N in Texas City, Tx with Frank and Florence Davison. And yes, the house she moved into was The Davison Home. According to a census taken in 1920, one year after the wedding, 6 people lived in the home at that time when the newlyweds moved in.

			—	house		daughter			F	W	28	
109	128	138	Davison Frank	Head		0	7	M	W	65	M
			— Florence	wife			7	W	57	M
			— Donald	son			M	W	18	M
			— Ida	daughter in law		7	W	45	M
			— Perry	son		M	W	17	S
			— Florence	daughter		7	W	15	S

Census Taken In 1920

Frank Davison, 65. Head of Household

Florence Davison, 57. Wife of Head

Donald Davison (The husband), 28. Son of Head

Ida Davison (The wife), 25. Daughter in Law of Head

Perry Davison, 17. Son of Head

Florence Davison, 15. Daughter of Head

At this time, Frank Davison was still operating the grocery store that he owned, and his son Donald was working at the family store alongside him learning the business. Don wasn't the oldest son of Frank, but he was the next in line to carry the torch for the family. Their family grocery store was opened in 1908, and it was in essence an extension of the grocery stores that the Davison family opened in Michigan. At first, Mr. Frank Davison operated the store inside of his home. The same home that Mrs. Ida Davison would eventually be attacked and murdered in.

In the early days of him creating this business, it was nothing to see patrons coming in and out of the house buying supplies and feed, but eventually Frank Davison was able to purchase a building for his store at 109 28th St in Texas City. Much like back home in Michigan, this became the family business. Everyone pitched in to keep the business afloat. This is why in 1920, the pioneering couple's oldest son, Don Davison, was still working at the grocery store with his father, and his mother and new wife were taking care of the home.

Ida and Don wasted no time getting pregnant and starting a family of their own. Almost exactly 9 months to the day after getting married in October of 1919, Ida Davison was giving birth to the couple's first child. At 9:15 p.m., on July 24, 1920, a beautiful baby girl was born. The couple decided to name her Mary Ella Davison. This child, who brought Ida so much joy when she came into the world, would unfortunately be the same child who would find Ida 50 years later lying on her kitchen floor covered in blood, just hours before Ida so violently left this world. **(See Photo 3A at the end of this chapter.)**

It would seem like Mary Ella's birth name paid homage to both sides of her family. 'Mary' was the first name of Ida's grandmother, and 'Ella' was the first name of Ida's mother. And of course, Davison was the family name that Ida married into. So, the name Mary Ella Davison was powerful in the sense that it tied multiple generations and multiple families together. This baby was truly a living symbol of the unity of two lives brought together for better or for worse, in sickness and in health.

The choice of names also shows the amount of love Don Davison had for his new wife. No doubt this name was constructed, at least in part, by Ida, and Don agreed. When honestly, in those days, the husband had exponentially more authority over household decisions than the wife. If he had not wanted that to be the name, it would not have been the name. But we can see a glimpse of his humility, love, and caring spirit by simply dissecting the name of their first child.

Four years later, on February 10, 1924, Don and Ida were once again blessed with another child. This time, the bundle of joy was a boy. His name was Donald Clinton Davison Jr. **(See Photo 4A at the end of this chapter.)** There is no need to guess at a breakdown of his name. He was named directly after his father. Perhaps this was because his father saw in him the man who would lead the family after his own death. A new generation of Davison's were beginning to fill up The Davison Home, and Ida saw all of her childhood dreams coming true.

By 1930, Mrs. Ida Davison was still living with her husband's parents at The Davison Home, but she was now working at the Davison and Co. grocery store with her husband. According to the records available, she was a sales lady at this time. Most likely she worked at the cash register and assisted their customers with finding the items they needed. Indeed, she was integrating into her new family quite well and doing everything she could to give her children the best life possible.

Also, in 1930 Ida joined the church that would become her church home until her death. She joined The First United Methodist Church in Texas City. Mrs. Ida Davison was so devoted to her denomination and her faith, that the very symbol of Methodism was engraved on her headstone. **(See Photo 5A at the end of this chapter.)** It was no surprise that Ida joined a Methodist church. Methodist was the denomination she was raised in. In fact, her father, Mr. W.E. Woodruff was a member of the Northside Methodist Church in Houston, and he was one of the founders of the old McKee Street Methodist Church of Houston.

By today's standards, many of us think that once a man and woman marry, they must move out of their parent's house and purchase a home of their own. However, in the early 1900's families were more closeknit than they are today. It was more beneficial to the elderly to have their children either living with them or very close by. What we know today as 'Old Folks' Homes' were a lot less common. Children took care of their parents when their parents could no longer take care of themselves. Ida knew that it would one day fall on her to become the woman of the house, and so she did everything in her power to prepare for this role with grace.

One of the main things that made the Davison family so prominent and well known was their commitment to improving the community around them. It was never about being the richest or most influential. It was never about ego. It was about humbly serving others, the giving of alms, supplying needs, and charity. It was about taking care of their family to the best of their ability and doing as much for their neighbors as they possibly could. Ida recognized this early on, and her naturally big heart helped her to fall into their pattern of selfless acts with ease.

In fact, in 1933 Ida helped to organize the Texas City Garden Club and she served as the very first president of the organization. Her mother-in-law, Mrs. Florence Davison, even hosted the very first meeting of this organization at The Davison Home. This showed the unity between the two women to better their community. The Texas City Garden Club still exists to this very day. The group focuses on teaching gardening to young women, hosting flower shows, and hosting events and projects that will help to beautify the city.

Mrs. Smithson Named Head Of Texas City Garden Club

TEXAS CITY — New officers of the Texas City Garden Club have been announced. President is Mrs. A. L. Smithson.

Serving with her are Mrs. Alton Pederson, first vice president; Mrs. Ward Gregory, second vice president; Mrs. L. A. Sadler, treasurer; Mrs. Leroy Schroeder, recording secretary; and Mrs. R. L. Argus, corresponding secretary.

Mrs. Jack O'Hara will serve as purchasing agent with Mrs. John Nichols, past president, as board member-at-large.

Members of the nominating committee were Mesdames M. E. Agee, J. B. Meyers, L. A. Sadler, R. J. Castanie, and Schroeder.

The club's honored guest at its meeting was Mrs. Don Davison, one of the charter members who helped organize the club in 1933 and served as first president.

Mrs. Harry Leach, program chairman, introduced the speaker, Mrs. Artis Davis of Webster, a national flower show judge. She entitled her demonstration of flower arranging "Take a Few Flowers." All foliage and flowers used in the 15 arrangements she did came from Mrs. Davis' yard.

Mrs. Davis used figurines in several arrangements, stressing that the figurine must be an integral part of the design, never just stuck in.

The regular monthly arrangements were brought by Mrs. B. H. Haxton and Mrs. P. J. Nessler and were judged by Mrs. Davis.

Mrs. M. E. Agee, study group chairman, announced a program for Feb. 15 and 16 at 9:30 a.m. in Nessler Civic Center. The program will be on design and color in flower arrangements.

Mrs. O'Hara, as purchasing agent, is taking orders for gladiola bulbs.

Galveston Daily News January 15, 1961

The club's honored guest at its meeting was Mrs. Don Davison, one of the charter members who helped organize the club in 1933 and served as first president.

41

Two years later, on February 21, 1935, at 8:15 a.m., tragedy struck The Davison Home. The original Davison of Texas City passed away, and the loss hit the family hard. Mr. Frank Davison was so influential that his death not only brought things in The Davison Home to a complete stop, but it also brought things in all of Texas City to complete stop as well. The government structure of Texas City literally went into mourning alongside the Davison family.

PIONEER RESIDENT OF MAINLAND DIES

FUNERAL SET TODAY FOR F.B. DAVISON, OLDEST TEXAS CITIAN.

Special to The News.

Texas City, Tex., Feb. 21.—Funeral services for Frank Burt Davison, 80, resident of Texas City for the past 41 years, who died at his home here this morning at 8:15 o'clock after a lingering illness, will be held Friday afternoon at 3 o'clock from the residence.

Rev. A. D. Lemons, pastor of the West End Methodist Church of Houston, will officiate, assisted by Rev. W. E. Hassler, pastor of the Texas City Central Methodist Church. Interment will be in the La Marque cemetery under the direction of H. B. Emken. Services at the grave will be under the auspices of Texas City Lodge No. 1118, A. F. and A. M.

A request that all Texas City business houses close their doors Friday afternoon between the hours of 3 and 4 p. m. in respect to Mr. Davison, who was a pioneer resident, was made today by Mayor Carl Nessler and City Commissioners M. E. Agee and W. P. Tarpey. Mr. Davison was a member of the first board of city commissioners here.

Galveston Daily News February 22, 1935

42

PIONEER RESIDENT OF MAINLAND DIES

FUNERAL SET TODAY FOR F.B. DAVISON, OLDEST TEXAS CITIAN.

Texas City, Tex., Feb. 21. – Funeral services for Frank Burt Davison, 80, resident of Texas City for the past 41 years, who died at his home here this morning at 8:15 o'clock after a lingering illness, will be held Friday afternoon at 3 o'clock from the residence.

Rev. A.D. Lemons, pastor of the West End Methodist Church of Houston, will officiate, assisted by Rev. W.E. Hassler, pastor of the Texas City Central Methodist Church. Interment will be in the La Marque cemetery under the direction of H.B. Emken. Services at the grave will be under the auspices of Texas City Lodge No 1118, A.F. and A.M.

A request that all Texas City businesses close their doors Friday afternoon between the hours of 3 and 4 p.m. in respect to Mr. Davison, who was a pioneer resident, was made today by Mayor Carl Nessler and City Commissioners...

After living for 80 years, and after doing more in one lifetime than many could do with several lifetimes, the Texas City powerhouse, pioneer, and oldest Texas Citian, Frank Davison, passed away inside of the home he himself had built. With his death, the entire dynamic at The Davison Home changed. Don Davison Sr. became the man of the house, the head of household, and the one who now controlled the family business. Likewise, his wife Ida Davison became the lady of the house, and a new generation of Davison's became the custodians of both the legacy of the Davison family, and The Davison Home itself.

In 1940, Ida was 45 years old, and she was no longer working at the grocery store. Instead, her 16-year-old son, Don Davison Jr. was working as a clerk at the family grocery store. Ida's primary job became caring for the home and tending to her community improvement activities. Mary Ella, her daughter, was 19 at the time and absent from the home. I am not sure where she was at this time or what she was doing.

						If child has not been given a first name. Enter Ⓧ after name of person furnishing information.						
1	2	3	4	5	6	7	8	A	9	10	11	12	13
41		29	R	13	No	Bell Willie Lee	Daughter		F	W	10	S	Yes
42						Adolph	Brother		M	W	38	S	No
43	109	40	0	7000	No	Davison Donald C	Head		M	W	48	M	No
44						Ida C Ⓧ	Wife		F	W	45	M	No
45						Mary Ella (AB	Daughter		F	W	19	S	Yes
46						Donald C. Jr	Son		M	W	16	S	Yes
47						Florence H	Mother		F	W	77	Wd	No
48	104	48	0	3000	No	Vogg Charles A	Head		M	W	49	M	No
49						Mildred M Ⓧ	Wife		F	W	36	M	No
50						Brock Franklin G	Lodger		M	W	50	Wd	No

Census Taken In 1940 Showing That Don Davison Was Now The Head Of The Household

One year later, on August 22, 1941, at 9:00 p.m., tragedy once again visited The Davison Home. The wife of the late Mr. Frank Davison, Mrs. Florence Davison, passed away and went on to be with her husband again in the afterlife.

Deaths

Services Today In Texas City For Mrs. Davison

Funeral services for Mrs. Florence Haven Davison, 78, wife of the late Frank B. Davison and a pioneer resident of Texas City, who died suddenly Friday, will be held this afternoon at 3 o'clock from her residence there, 107 3d Ave.

Rev. F. Clyde Woodward, pastor of the First Methodist Church of Texas City, will officiate, and interment will be in La Marque Cemetery.

Survivors are: Five daughters, Mrs. Mary McClintock, Mrs. Gene Kilgore and Mrs. Christine Jones, all of Texas City, Mrs. Margaret Grainger of Houston, and Mrs. Florence Hart of Goose Creek; three sons, George Orrie Davison and Donald Clinton Davison, both of Texas City, and Perry Allen Davison, Amityville, N. Y.; 25 grandchildren, eight great-grandchildren and other relatives.

Galveston Daily News August 24, 1941

"Services Today In Texas City For Mrs. Davison"

Funeral services for Mrs. Florence Haven Davison, 78, wife of the late Frank B. Davison and a pioneer resident of Texas City, who died suddenly Friday, will be held this afternoon at 3 o'clock from her residence there, 109 3rd Ave.

After 78 years of life, Mrs. Florence Davison's time on earth finally came to an end, and Rev. F. Clyde Woodward, pastor of the First Methodist Church of Texas City officiated the funeral. Just like her husband, she took her last breaths in this world inside of the home that she and her late husband built. Even in death, both Frank and Florence will be together for all eternity. Also, when one looks at the symbols on the far left and far right of their joint headstone, we can see that not only was Mr. Frank Davison a Mason, as indicated by the compass and square next to his name, we also see that Mrs. Florence Davison was an Eastern Star, as indicated by the five-pointed star next to her name.

Headstone Of Frank And Florence Davison

Just to make this make sense, the Masons are an exclusively male organization. The wives of Masons are generally members of a group known as The Eastern Stars. Not all wives of Masons are in this group, however. But the simplest way to understand it, without me going too far off topic to break it all down, is to just simply say that The Eastern Stars are like the female version of the Masons.

One month after the passing of Florence Davison, Ida Davison was now the uncontested lady of The Davison Home, she was 47 years old, she was married with two children, and her primary occupation was taking care of her home and her family. It would appear that everything in life was going her way, and Ida was truly living the dream. Along with her husband, she owned a three-story home, a successful grocery store, and she was active in her community.

At this time Ida was a member of the Texas City Garden Club, the First United Methodist Church in Texas City, she was a part of the church's youth program, she was a member of the Women's Society of Christian Service, and she was also a member of the Bocker Sunday School Class. Mrs. Ida Davison truly dedicated her life to her family, her church, and her community, and she was always available to speak with someone who needed wise counsel, helpful advice, and spiritual guidance.

In 1950, Mrs. Ida Davison's services were once again needed at the family grocery store, and as usual, she rose to the occasion. She began doing the work of an accountant for the business and also working as a cashier. It was her job to keep the books and balance the budget. This didn't mean that her duties at home disappeared. On the contrary. She took on these responsibilities at the store in addition to her responsibilities at home. Some of her duties at home were easier seeing how at this time, both of her children were grown and out of the house.

For the next 20 years, Mrs. Ida Davison took care of her home, did work in her community, stayed connected with her children and grandchildren, stayed faithful to her church home, loved her husband unconditionally, and did her best to do everything as right as any woman could do it. She was loved by many, spoken highly of in multiple circles, and had successfully navigated her existence on planet earth better than most.

So now, we must ask the question again. How did such a sweet, kind, and caring woman end up brutally beaten bleeding out on her very own kitchen floor? Why would someone want her dead? Who could be so cruel that they would perpetrate what is now known as the most infamous murder in Texas City history on such a gentle soul?

Photo 1A

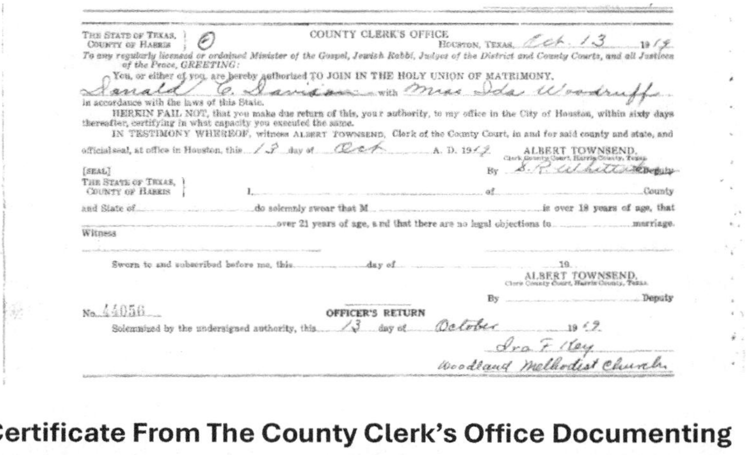

Certificate From The County Clerk's Office Documenting The Marriage Of Donald Davison And Ida Woodruff

The State of Texas
County of Harris

To any regularly licensed or ordained Minister of the Gospel, Jewish Rabbi, Judge of the District and County Courts, and all Justices of the Peace—Greetings:

YOU, OR EITHER OF YOU, ARE HEREBY
AUTHORIZED TO JOIN

In the Holy Union of Matrimony

Donald C. Davison
with
Miss Ida Woodruff
In Accordance with the Laws of this State

Herein Fail Not, that you make due return of this, your authority, to my office in the City of Houston, within sixty days thereafter, certifying in what capacity you executed the same.

In Testimony Whereof, witness Albert Townsend, Clerk of the County Court in said County and State, and official Seal at office in Houston, this 13 day of Oct., A. D. 1919

ALBERT TOWNSEND,
Clerk County Court, Harris County, Texas.

By S. R. Whitaker Deputy

Officer's Return

Solemnized by the undersigned authority this 13 day of October 1919

No. 44056
Book 21 Page 42

Ira F. Key
Woodland Methodist Church

Marriage License Of Don Davison And Ida Woodruff

Photo 3A

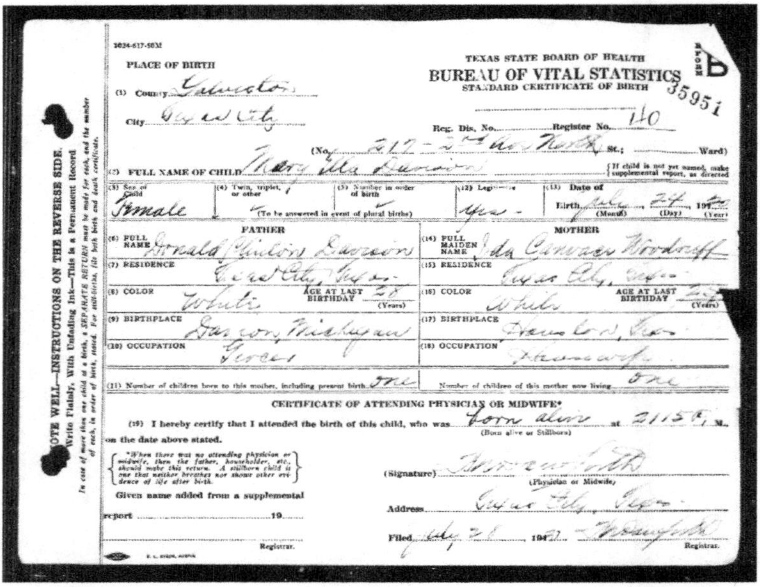

Birth Certificate Of Mary Ella Davison (Mary Ella Opersteny)

Photo 4A

Birth Certificate Of Donald Clinton Davison Jr

Photo 5A

**Headstone Of Don And Ida Davison Showing The Symbols
For Masonry And Methodism**

Chapter 4

How Mrs. Ida Davison Died

Texas City Woman, 75, Murdered

By JERRY COOPER
NEWS STAFF WRITER

TEXAS CITY — Intruders fatally beat an elderly member of a pioneer Texas City family in her home at 109 3rd Ave. North between 7:45 a.m. and 9:40 a.m. Saturday.

Mrs. Don C. (Ida) Davison, 75, died about noon Saturday at Galveston County Memorial Hospital where she was taken after being discovered bleeding from head wounds in the kitchen of her home by her daughter and son - in - law, Mr. and Mrs. E. J. Opersteny.

"There was certainly a homicide there and we're investigating it now," Texas City Police Chief Rankin DeWalt said Saturday afternoon.

DeWalt said a medical examination is being conducted by the Galveston County Medical Examiner's office in an effort to determine a motive for the fatal beating. He said there were no signs of a struggle and the house was "neat" when officers arrived.

He said that a purse on the kitchen table did not seem to be disturbed, but the family hadn't had a chance to see if anything was missing.

Mr. Davison told police he left his wife "working around the house as usual" when he went to work at about 7:45 a.m. Shortly before Mrs. Davison was discovered seriously injured, her daughter had tried to call her and getting no answer had gone by to see about her.

Funeral services will be held at 4:30 p.m. Monday at the First United Methodist Church, the Rev. Edwin Summers officiating. Burial will be in La Marque Cemetery.

Mrs. Davison was born Sept. 30, 1894, in Houston. She was a member of both the Women's Society of Christian Service and the Booker Sunday School Class at the First United Methodist Church where she worked many years in the church's youth program. She belonged to the church for 40 years.

She lived for more than 50 years in the Davison house at 109 3rd Ave. North. The house bears a state of Texas historical plaque.

Mrs. Davison and her husband celebrated their fiftieth wedding anniversary on Oct. 12 last year.

Besides her husband and daughter, survivors include three sisters, Mrs. Ella F. Medley of Houston, Mrs. Kate Sims of Houston and Mrs. Myrtle Haydel of California; and three grandchildren.

In lieu of flowers, the family asked that donations be made to the First United Methodist Church Memorial Fund.

Galveston Daily News September 20, 1970

Texas City Woman, 75, Murdered

Texas City – Intruders fatally beat an elderly member of a pioneer Texas City family in her home at 109 3rd Ave North between 7:45 a.m. and 9:40 a.m. Saturday.

Mrs. Don C. (Ida) Davison, 75, died about noon Saturday at Galveston County Memorial Hospital where she was taken after being discovered bleeding from head wounds in the kitchen of her home by her daughter and son-in-law, Mr. and Mrs. E.J. Opersteny.

"There was certainly a homicide there and we're investigating it now," Texas City Police Chief Rankin DeWalt said Saturday afternoon.

DeWalt said a medical examination is being conducted by the Galveston County Medical Examiner's office in an effort to determine a motive for the fatal beating. He said there were no signs of a struggle, and the house was "neat" when officers arrived.

He said that a purse on the kitchen table did not seem to be disturbed, but the family hadn't had a chance to see if anything was missing.

Mr. Davison told police he left his wife "working around the house as usual" when he went to work at about 7:45 a.m. Shortly before Mrs. Davison was discovered seriously injured, her daughter had tried to call her and getting no answer had gone by to see about her.

Funeral services will be held at 4:30 p.m. Monday at the First United Methodist Church, the Rev. Edwin Summers officiating. Burial will be in La Marque Cemetery.

Mrs. Davison was born Sept. 30, 1984, in Houston. She was a member of both the Women's Society of Christian Service and the Bocker Sunday School Class at the First United Methodist Church where she worked many years in the church's youth program. She belonged to the church for 40 years.

She lived for more than 50 years in The Davison Home at 109 3rd Ave North. The house bears a state of Texas historical plaque.

Mrs. Davison and her husband celebrated their fiftieth wedding anniversary on Oct. 12 last year.

Besides her husband and daughter, survivors include three sisters, Mrs. Ella F. Medley of Houston, Mrs. Kate Sims of Houston, and Mrs. Myrtle Haydel of California; and three grandchildren.

In lieu of flowers, the family asked that donations be made to the First United Methodist Church Memorial Fund.

So, what actually happened to Mrs. Ida Davison that fateful Saturday morning back in 1970? Well, based on the facts that I was able to uncover while researching this case, I feel confident that I can piece together for you the events which unfolded on September 19, 1970.

The morning began much like countless other mornings had begun for Ida. By this time, the only two people who were living at The Davison Home were Don and Ida. The couple woke up together around the same time, probably around 6 or 7 a.m., took care of their daily hygienic routines, and commenced to preparing for their day. At the time, Don was still running the family grocery store he had inherited from his father Frank, so that morning he spent his time drinking coffee and getting ready for work.

Ida, on the other hand, was no longer active at the store. Her primary job was that of a housewife. As her husband of over 50 years got ready to go and provide for her, she slipped into something more comfortable. Something that she could wear around the house while she cleaned and enjoyed the life she had built for herself.

Her around the house attire was simple. She wore a brown hair net upon her head, a white slip covering her delicate 170 lbs. frame, and a pink and white striped housecoat over her slip. It is possible that everything other than the housecoat is actually what she was wearing while she slept the night before. Knowing that the Galveston Daily News made their newspaper deliveries around 3:00 a.m. every morning, Ida walked out of her front door and stepped outside into the fresh Texas City air looking for the day's newspaper.

The sun was just beginning to shine, the weather was favorable, and there was cool breeze coming off of the Gulf, swirling around her and lightly blowing her housecoat to and fro. Ida stood there for a few moments on her beautiful, covered porch, and as was her habit, she thanked God for her many blessings. Then, she walked down her steps, picked up the newspaper and made her way back inside. The way the paper was rolled up in its plastic bag cover made it possible to only read the headline for the day.

Galveston Daily News September 19, 1970

Ida wasn't exactly what one would call a sports fanatic, but she was no doubt happy to see that the Texas City High School football team had defeated St. Thomas 9 – 0, in their latest game. Walking into her kitchen, she sat the newspaper down on the table and started a pot of coffee. Around 7:45 a.m., she kissed her husband goodbye and followed him as he walked towards the back door. Don usually kept his car parked out back in the driveway directly behind the kitchen door.

Ida stood in the doorway holding the screen door open with one hand, and waved goodbye with the other as Don pulled out of the driveway and headed to work. Neither of them knew that they were saying goodbye to each other for the last time. If they did, perhaps they would have held each other tighter and longer. Perhaps they would've kissed each other more deeply and passionately. Perhaps they would have peered deep into each other's eyes as if they were looking directly into their souls and took the time to tell each other all of the things that people wish they would've said if they knew they would never see the love of their life again.

Once Don was gone, Ida closed the screen door behind her, but she did not lock the latch, and she left the inner wooden door wide open. She also walked to the front of her home and did the same thing. She opened the inner wooden door but left the screen door closed and unlocked. It would appear that she did this to let the air from outside flow through the house and cool it down, and also to let the sunlight in. This saved on electricity, and it was a normal practice in 1970.

Going back into the kitchen, Ida sat down at the table, continued drinking her coffee, and flipped through the pages of the newspaper. What exactly did she decide to read, though? We cannot be 100% sure of exactly which pages she chose to read but we can imagine in our minds what those pages might have been. Most of us scan through the various pages until we find something that interests us. We can rightfully assume that Ida did the same thing. So, we are left with a question. What would you have read that morning while you sipped your coffee and prepared for the day?

Would you have turned to the section which contained the latest Dear Abby letter?

Dear Abby . . .

Unwed Mother Asks: Is It Wrong To Give Baby Away?

By Abigail Van Buren

DEAR ABBY: To start out with, I am an unwed mother. I kept my baby. Bobby is six months old now and is very sweet, but I don't feel I can give him the love and attention I should. You see, I work eight hours a day in a restaurant. It doesn't pay much. At night I usually have a date. I live with my family and they take care of Bobby. My father sort of shames me when I mention giving Bobby away. The only reason I kept the baby was I thought I would get his father to marry me. I am only 17 and want to live like other kids my age.

The boys have no respect for me and my girl friends let me know that they are better than me.

I would like to go back to school in another town and maybe start over again. Would it be so terrible to give my baby away? My folks can't give him much, and I think that giving him away would be the best way of showing him that I really loved him. CONFUSED

DEAR CONFUSED: I see your point, and appreciate your confusion, but let's consider the baby. An unwanted child is rarely fooled. He knows he is unwanted and he'll suffer because of it. Perhaps your parents love and want Bobby enough to raise him. They may not be able to provide him with material things, but if he is given love, he'll be all right.

You are honest to admit that you don't want the child, and think he deserves better. Perhaps giving him away is the solution. Talk it over with your parents.

DEAR ABBY: You deserve 10 lashes with a wet diaper for condoning the "Mamma doll" who actually gives birth to a "baby doll." Good grief, is nothing sacred?

DISAPPOINTED IN S. C.

What's your problem? You'll feel better if you get it off your chest. Write to ABBY, Box 69700, Los Angeles, Cal. 90069. For a personal reply enclose stamped, addressed envelope.

Galveston Daily News September 19, 1970

Dear Abby... Unwed Mother Asks: Is It Wrong To Give Baby Away?

DEAR ABBY: To start out with, I am an unwed mother. I kept my baby. Bobby is six months old now and is very sweet, but I don't feel I can give him the love and attention I should. You see, I work eight hours a day in a restaurant. It

doesn't pay much. At night I usually have a date. I live with my family and they take care of Bobby. My father sort of shames me when I mention giving Bobby away. The only reason I kept the baby was I thought I would get his father to marry me. I am only 17 and want to live like other kids my age.

The boys have no respect for me and my girl friends let me know that they are better than me.

I would like to go back to school in another town and maybe start over again. Would it be so terrible to give my baby away? My folks can't give him much, and I think that giving him away would be the best way of showing him that I really loved him.

CONFUSED

DEAR CONFUSED: I see your point, and appreciate your confusion, but let's consider the baby. An unwanted child is rarely fooled. He knows he is unwanted and he'll suffer because of it. Perhaps your parents love and want Bobby enough to raise him. They may not be able to provide him with material things, but if he is given love, he'll be all right.

You are honest to admit that you don't want the child, and think he deserves better. Perhaps giving him away is the solution. Talk it over with your parents.

DEAR ABBY: You deserve 10 lashes with a wet diaper for condoning the "Mamma doll" who actually gives birth to a "baby doll". Good grief, is nothing sacred?

DISAPPOINTED IN S.C.

What's your problem? You'll feel better if you get it off your chest. Write to ABBY, Box 69700, Los Angelos, Cal. 90069. For a personal reply enclose stamped, addressed envelope.

Or would you have turned to the section of the paper with the daily horoscope? Many people like to read their daily horoscope message in an attempt to garner some glimpse into their individual future. If Ida had done this, what would she have found? What would she have interpreted its meaning to be? Being born on September 30th, her sign would have been Libra. Libra, the seventh sign in the zodiac, belongs to those born between the dates of September 23rd to October 22nd.

Libras are said to be intelligent, kind, and always willing to put others before themselves. Libras value harmony in all forms. Ruled by Venus, the planet of beauty, Libra adores a life that looks good. As the master of compromise and diplomacy, Libra is adept at seeing all points of view and excels at crafting compromises and effecting mediation between others. This sign has a rich inner life yet loves other people, and they're always happiest with a large group of friends, family, and coworkers on whom they can count.

That sounds like it describes the late Mrs. Ida C. Davison to a "T". Let's read what Ida would've read if she did in fact decide to read her horoscope that morning.

stress your sense of values and
aim only for the worthwhile.

SEPT. 24 to OCT. 23 (Libra) —
Lesser matters are highlighted
now, but these may spark big
achievements later. So,
whatever you attempt, give your
best. Be prepared for all
contingencies.

OCT. 24 to NOV. 22 (Scorpio)

Galveston Daily News September 19, 1970

Sept. 24 to Oct. 23 (Libra) –

Lesser matters are highlighted now, but these may spark big achievements later. So, whatever you attempt, give your best. Be prepared for all contingencies.

They always say that hindsight is 20/20 and that may very well be true. Perhaps when we are looking back at a situation that took place in the past, we can more easily see omens and signs than the person who experienced that situation in real time. For instance, when I read over this horoscope that Ida would have read the morning of her murder, I can see clear warnings about the horrors to come.

"Lesser matters are highlighted now, but these may spark big achievements later."

Could this be applied to her seemingly small decision to leave her doors unlocked and opened? If this is something that she did every day, it would most definitely be a matter of less importance, however, the consequences of such an action on this day in particular could make it easier for her killer to gain entrance to the home.

"So, whatever you attempt, give your best."

We know that Ida was attacked. Perhaps this is trying to tell her that when she attempts to fight off her attacker she should give it her best shot. Why? Because this fight will quite literally be a life-or-death fight.

"Be prepared for all contingencies."

Most of the time, we do not have a plan for when things go bad. We get lulled into a sense of complacency when things are going good for us. We tend to think bad things happen to bad people, or at the very least, bad things happen to everyone else, but not us. How often do you read about a murder in the newspaper or on social media and you honestly believe that you yourself might lose your life in the same way? Which one of you reading this book thinks that they will leave this earth, how Mrs. Ida Davison did? Most likely none of you are thinking this same thing will happen to you one day.

That statement in her horoscope seems as if it could be telling Ida to be prepared for anything to happen that day. Even the thing that she least suspects. And if the unexpected does happen, she should fight like hell to make it out of the situation. But like I said earlier, hindsight is always 20/20. Most likely Ida would not have seen that horoscope how we see it today. We have the benefit of knowing the dark deeds that are about to take place. Unfortunately, Mrs. Ida Davison was totally caught off guard.

While researching this book, I also took the time to see what my own horoscope said that day. Even though I would not be born for another 12 years, my curiosity got the best of me. This is what I found.

Make some time for relaxation.
AUGUST 24 to SEPT. 23
(Virgo) — Mild planetary influences. This day will be largely what you make of it. Stress your sense of values and aim only for the worthwhile.
SEPT 24 to OCT 23 (Libra) —

Galveston Daily News September 19, 1970

August 24 to Sept. 23 (Virgo) –

Mild planetary influences. This day will be largely what you make of it. Stress your sense of values and aim only for the worthwhile.

Even though I was not born when this particular horoscope was written, I can't help but find wisdom within its words for myself as the author of this work. Let me explain. I did not wake up one morning and simply decide to write a true crime novel about Texas City's most infamous murder. In fact, I never once thought about writing a true crime novel about any murders at all. Although I have written 16 novels prior to this one in several different genres, true crime has never really been on my radar.

The initial idea that eventually evolved into the book you are reading began with me wanting to write a horror story. I wanted to write a horror novel, and so I began writing a story about ghosts, ghouls, demons, and the occult. While researching for my horror novel, I asked the general public about the ghost stories they had heard in reference to The Davison Home. Why? The Davison Home was going to be the central location for my tale of haunted phenomenon.

When the public began to respond, one person in particular mentioned a murder that happened at The Davison Home in the past. I had never heard about this murder before, but I thought it would be good for my novel. I figured I could tie the origins of my ghost to a real-life murder and mix fantasy and fiction in an impactful way. So, I naturally began researching this murder to confirm that it actually happened, but to also learn some of the details.

As I researched it, I became enamored with the details. I found a few newspaper clippings describing the murder, so I knew that it was real, but from what I read, something did not sit well with me. I began to think that perhaps the police had arrested the wrong suspect, and the real killer was allowed to go free. I love a good conspiracy. I thought that I found a conspiracy from the past, and my intentions for my book shifted.

Instead of writing a horror novel, I figured I could write a novel about a man who was falsely accused of murder and give my theory on who the actual murderer was. I then began writing my new book and doing research on it. The more research I did, however, the more convinced I became that the man who was arrested for the crime was without a doubt the man who committed the crime. So again, I scraped my book idea, and I followed the evidence.

The evidence led me to the book that I am writing now. I felt as if I were being led to tell the story of this wonderful woman and give the public the facts pertaining to the case that has never been viewed by the general public. I believe that the truth is more important than anything else, and in all things that we do, we must strive to do that which is good.

To me, that ties in with the phrase in the horoscope, *"This day will be largely what you make of it"*. That means that as the author I can craft any story out of this day that I want. It can be whatever I make of it. I can make it a horror story. I can make it a conspiracy theory about an innocent man convicted of a crime he didn't commit. Or I could make it a true crime narrative and tell the real story exactly as it is and let the chips fall where they may.

Also, the statement in the horoscope, *"Stress your sense of values and aim only for the worthwhile"*, feels like a direct statement to me. It is telling me that when I endeavor to tell the story of Mrs. Ida Davison, I must do so in a manner which aligns with my values. By nature, I am a humble man. I am a man who believes in doing what is right. I am a man that is willing to change my mind and opinion when exposed to new information and evidence. So naturally, I am a man who will scrap any book idea that is based on false assumptions and try my best to write a book based on the facts and the facts alone. Indeed, doing that which is right is the only thing which is worthwhile. It is amazing how me as the author has a connection to the deceased through the newspaper horoscope she would have read the morning of her death.

Or perhaps, she skipped over the horoscope page completely and turned instead to the comic strip section of the newspaper that morning. Everyone likes to read a good comic strip. But what exactly would she have seen if she turned to the comic strips?

Galveston Daily News September 19, 1970

Or maybe she scanned over the TV listings and made plans to watch the debut of the Mary Tyler Moore Show.

Galveston Daily News September 19, 1970

While it's true that we can't be sure what all Ida read that morning, we can be sure about this. Sadly, it was the last thing she ever read.

Her husband left for work around 7:45 a.m. Just a short 15 minutes later, around 8:00 a.m., her killer was prowling around the outside of her home peeking in through the windows with criminality and savagery on his mind. Looking around to ensure that he was not being watched, the killer then crept up the steps of Ida's porch and peered in through the screen door. Realizing that the screen door was unlocked, he then carefully opened it up, trying to be as quiet as possible, and entered through the front door. Then, he silently made his way through the home searching for things that he could steal. After all, The Davison Home was the largest home in the area and the family name had come to be associated with prestige and wealth.

Making his way towards the kitchen, the killer found himself creeping up behind his victim. Ida was still sitting down at the kitchen table with her newspaper laid out in front of her when she heard the footsteps behind her. Turning around to see if perhaps her husband had returned home for some reason, Ida came face to face with the intruder. The only thing she had time to do was scream one time before a heavy fist crashed down into her face with the overwhelming force of a 6'5 fully grown man.

The blow knocked the elderly woman over and her head slammed into the table causing blood to spray onto the table and the newspaper. Disoriented, Mrs. Ida Davison fell out of her chair and collapsed onto the floor. She could feel the room begin to spin and she fought as hard as she could to maintain consciousness. She was no doubt experiencing a wide range of emotions and thoughts.

First and foremost, she would have been experiencing breathtaking fear. Second, she would have been wondering who her attacker was and questioning why they were attacking her. It is possible that she recognized the intruder from the quick glimpse that she got, but we cannot know this for sure. Also, the pain that would have been zigzagging through her body must have been excruciating. Most of our elders are in some form of constant pain just due to old age. Couple that with a swift blow to the head and a fall from a kitchen chair, she was no doubt suffering greatly.

As she lay there, possibly moaning and writhing in pain, the savage intruder did not come to his senses, realize the error of his ways, and flee the scene.

No!

Instead, the intruder doubled down on his reprehensible behavior. Kneeling down over his victim, he preceded to deliver blow after blow to the head and face of the helpless woman. His intentions were clear. From all of the evidence available to us, he was trying to beat this poor woman to death. Who knows where all of this anger and rage came from? And who knows why he unleashed it on such an innocent victim? The only conclusion we can draw is that the culprit was one of the worst types of people that society could produce. The kind that had no empathy for those around them.

Mrs. Ida fought back as best she could. She pushed, scratched, and clawed at her attacker, but her 75-year-old frame could not muster up enough strength to mount an effective defense. At some point during the relentless beating, Mrs. Ida Davison had fought as hard as she possibly could, but because of the head wounds she had suffered, she eventually went unconscious.

Perhaps this was in some way a blessing. Her body may have suffered so much shock and pain that it simply shut down in order to spare her from feeling the extreme brutality. When she finally stopped moving, and began to barely breathe, the intruder stood over her body and examined her. In his mind, he had successfully finished the job, and she lay there dead.

He looked around the kitchen and examined his handiwork. There was blood on the table, blood on the newspaper, blood on the wall next to the body, blood on the head and face of his victim, and a pool of blood coalescing beneath her head from the wounds which he inflicted. There were even three human teeth laying next to the body which he had knocked out of her mouth with his bare hands. Adrenaline and evil intentions surged through his mind and body as he viewed his handiwork.

He stood there for a moment and contemplated searching the house for valuables, but the demon which he was, was not yet through with Mrs. Ida. As he looked at her lying helplessly on her kitchen floor, and assuming in his own twisted mind that she was dead, he felt a strange sensation tingling in his nether regions. A crooked smile slowly formed on his face and a bulge began to grow in his shorts. Grunting softly, the intruder began massaging his member as he looked down at the bloody grandmother.

Glancing around the kitchen he considered his predicament. He was already guilty of breaking and entering, and he was already guilty of murder. Why not, he thought, do everything he ever wanted to do? Why not live out every sick, twisted, and insane fantasy that he ever had? After all, a dead body could not tell him "No" and a dead body could not stop him from violating it. It didn't matter that he was looking at a bloody body. It didn't matter that he was looking at a pillar of the community. It didn't matter that he was looking at a 75-year-old mother and grandmother. To him, he was only looking at a piece of meat. There was no humanity inside of him, so he could not see the humanity in Mrs. Ida.

"Fuck it!" The intruder mumbled under his breath, giving his manhood one last good squeeze as it reached full size.

Kneeling down, he lifted up the house coat and the white slip that Mrs. Ida was wearing, and he pulled her panties down and off of her legs. Tossing them to the side, he unzipped his shorts and exposed himself through the hole in his underwear. Then, going against everything that is decent and good, he penetrated his victim as she lay there unconscious and assaulted her in the vilest way imaginable. We can only thank God that at this point Mrs. Ida was still unconscious, and she had no knowledge of the humiliation and disgusting violation that she was enduring. The intruder assaulted her with no mercy. He was so rough with her lifeless body that he caused her vagina to bleed.

After the sexual assault, it appears that the intruder then went on to forage through the refrigerator searching for a bite to eat, showing a complete disregard for the crime he had committed and the elderly woman he had viciously victimized. Perhaps he found a snack and perhaps he did not. But, after checking for food, he then went from room to room throughout the three-story home looking for money and valuables that he could steal. Finding about $4 worth of change, he placed his ill-gotten gains into his pockets and continued his search.

While he searched, the intruder thought he heard Mrs. Ida moaning softly in the kitchen and it was at that point he realized she was not dead. Becoming afraid, the intruder dropped what he was doing and gasped. He thought that if his victim were waking up, she could possibly start screaming for help, and he might be trapped inside of the home when the police arrived. Deciding to give up his search for money and valuables, he sprinted out the front door, the same door which he had entered through, and disappeared into the alleyways of Texas City. Then, he made his escape away from the scene of the crime. As he fled, the realization of what he done began to set it, but the intruder still felt absolutely no remorse.

For almost two hours, Mrs. Ida Davison laid there alone on her kitchen floor bleeding from her head and her vaginal area. She was dying an extremely slow and excruciating death. It wouldn't be until around 9:42 a.m. that her daughter and son-in-law would drive around to The Davison Home to check on her and ultimately make the gruesome discovery that would lead to that faithful 911 call. And as stated earlier, that 911 call would alter the history of Texas City forever.

Chapter 5

The Texas City Police Department Conducts Their Investigation

As stated earlier, the first two officers to arrive at the crime scene were Officer Henry and Officer Oliver. After family members and neighbors informed them where they could locate the female victim in need of assistance, these two men entered the home, and were caught totally off guard by the horrors they encountered within. This pair did not begin to process the crime scene, however. Their first job was to check and see if Mrs. Ida Davison was still breathing and perform life-saving measures until the ambulance arrived.

They also secured the location, made sure the suspect was not hiding out somewhere within the residence, and began taking statements from all of the neighbors while their memories of the morning's events were fresh in their minds. One of the officers, Officer Deril Oliver, was extremely traumatized by what he was witnessing. At this time, he had been a police officer with the City of Texas City for about 8 years, but he had known Mrs. Ida Davison personally for about 20 years. He could not believe what he was seeing, and he wanted desperately for her to survive this ordeal. He also made a vow to himself that he was going to do everything in his power to catch the person responsible.

Soon after the police arrived on the scene, the Crowder Ambulance Service showed up and transported the still unconscious victim to County Memorial Hospital in West Texas City. Police Chief Rankin DeWalt also arrived on the scene with Texas City's first ever Hispanic police officer, Lt. Saragoza. According to the official reports, it was Lt. Saragoza who processed the crime scene while Chief DeWalt gave out orders to his police force to look underneath every rock and follow every lead until the person who committed this crime was in custody.

As the Texas City Police Department scoured the city and searched for leads on a suspect, Lt. Saragoza meticulously went through The Davison Home with a fine-tooth comb, collecting evidence and taking photographs that would be helpful in not only identifying the suspect who committed this crime, but also to convict them in a court of law once they were caught.

According to the official reports, an investigation of the crime scene indicated that the victim was possibly sitting at the kitchen table when attacked. A newspaper which was on the table had blood on the corner of it, which indicated the victim had fallen face down onto it. A woman's black purse was on the table, but it did not appear to have been disturbed.

There was a coffee cup on the table which showed traces of what appeared to be coffee inside of it. A toaster, located next to the stove, which is south of the table, had two pieces of bread in the raised position which were still soft. It looked as if someone had placed the bread inside the toaster but for some reason did not press it down to allow it to toast. There was a large amount of water on the floor which appeared to have come from an overflowing sink. One side of the sink was filled to the top and the other side was filled approximately halfway with water. Perhaps Ida was filling the sink up with water so that she could wash dishes after reading the newspaper but was attacked before she could do this and the water simply continued to run.

On the floor near the sink, in the water, lay a pair of white female underpants. It was noted that the crotch of the underpants had been ripped, and assuming that they belonged to the victim, Lt. Saragoza placed the underpants into evidence. A human tooth was found near the table, and another tooth was found in the blood under the head of the victim, and yet another tooth was found on the floor next to the victim's head. Those three human teeth, presumably belonging to the victim, were placed into evidence. Lt. Saragoza also found some hair at the scene that did not seem to belong to the victim, and he placed that into evidence as well.

He found hair that appeared to be hair from the head of a possible suspect, and hair that appeared to be pubic hair from a possible suspect. Lt. Saragoza also found grass on the kitchen floor, so he placed that into evidence, and he also took a sample of grass from the yard. His thought process seems to have been that the grass from inside the home could be tested later and it could be determined whether or not the grass inside of the home came from the actual yard of The Davison Home or some other source.

The investigation concluded that there was no indication of a struggle in the kitchen. This meant that the victim went down to the ground relatively fast without being able to put up much of a fight. There were also no indications that anything else in the house had been disturbed, however, the family had not yet been allowed to search the residence to check if anything was out of place or missing.

The initial examination of the crime scene didn't really point to a specific suspect, nor a motive, but it did reveal some very telling clues about how the crime took place. In order to find out who did it and why, the police needed to actually hit the streets. One of the first things they did was go door to door and find out if any of the neighbors saw or heard anything suspicious that morning. From the timeline provided by Mrs. Opersteny, the police knew that the crime took place sometime between 7:45 a.m. when Mr. Davison left to go to work, and 9:42 a.m. when Mrs. Davison was found incapacitated. This gave the police a narrow window of just about two hours to focus on.

The neighborhood check was conducted by four Texas City Police Officers. They were the two officers who first responded to the crime scene, Officer Henry and Officer Oliver, and these two were joined by Officer Eden and Officer Gilmore. These four officers spread out and conducted their investigation. Officer Oliver spoke with a group of small children who lived in a house across the alley behind The Davison Home. These children told him that earlier that day they heard the Davison's dog barking; however, they did not see anyone around the house.

Unfortunately for the police, the children did not provide an approximate time when this occurred. They were only able to confirm that it happened earlier than 9:42 a.m. when Mr. and Mrs. Opersteny arrived. Perhaps it was suspect trying to enter the home. Or perhaps it was the suspect trying to flee from the home. Or perhaps, it was simple a dog barking a bird or a squirrel.

Another neighbor that was interviewed who had a small morsel of information to share was a man named Mr. Edward Swann who lived at 204 1st St N. He lived directly across the street from Rev. Ruefenacht's church. Mr. Edward Swann stated that shortly prior to 8:00 a.m. he heard what he thought was a scream, but he thought it was either children playing or someone having a family argument. That is interesting because even though he reported hearing someone scream; he did not explicitly state that the scream sounded like a woman.

He even said that he assumed the scream was associated with a family argument. It could easily be assumed that if his thoughts were correct, there could have been an argument between Mrs. Ida Davison and her husband Mr. Don C. Davison, just before he claimed to have left to go to work. In fact, most murders are committed by someone who knows the victim personally. A recent study concluded that around 60 percent of women murdered are murdered by their partners or a close family member.

During the neighborhood check, the officers also spoke with Rev. Ruefenacht again. When they did, he stated that at approximately 8:30 a.m. he was in the alley behind The Davison Home looking for his dog. However, he also said that he did not see or hear anything unusual. So, an hour before he made the 911 call, he was in the alley between his church and The Davison Home, and at that time, he did not see nor hear anything suspicious.

At this point, the police were trying to construct a timeline of events that would prove valuable in the days to come, but they still didn't have a suspect. What they needed was a witness. Either a witness to the crime, a witness to a suspicious person lurking around The Davison Home that morning, or a witness who saw someone suspicious fleeing the scene. Before we continue, let us look at the timeline that was constructed from the neighborhood check.

7:45 a.m. – Mr. Don C. Davison, the last person to see the victim before the assault, leaves his home at 109 3rd Ave. N.

Unknown Time – A group of small children hear the Davison's Dog barking, but they do not see anyone around The Davison Home.

7:55 a.m. – Mr. Edward Swann hears someone scream.

8:30 a.m. – Rev. Ruefenacht goes into the alley between his church and The Davison Home to search for his dog, but he does not see or hear anything unusual.

9:00 a.m. – Mrs. Opersteny makes a phone call to her mother, but she receives no answer.

9:00 a.m. – 9:30 a.m. – Mrs. Opersteny makes several more phone calls to her mother, Mrs. Davison, but none of her phone calls are answered.

9:30 a.m. – Mrs. Opersteny becomes worried and decides to drive over to her mother's home to check on her.

9:42 a.m. – Mr. and Mrs. Opersteny arrive at The Davison Home, they see the victim lying in a pool of blood, and they call out to the neighbors to call for help.

9:42 a.m. – Rev. Ruefenacht calls the Texas City Police Department and request an ambulance and the police. He states that a woman has been badly hurt at The Davison Home.

This basic timeline told police one of two things happened. Either Mr. Don Davison was the person who assaulted Mrs. Ida Davison prior to leaving for work, or the actual suspect entered the home shortly after Mr. Davison left for work and committed the crime. I'm sure the police considered both of these scenarios, but I would suspect that they quickly ruled out the idea that Mr. Davison was the culprit. The pair had been married for over 50 years, and there had never been any indication that their marriage was anything but a loving marriage. Plus, it could easily be verified if Mr. Davison showed up to open the grocery store on time, and if he looked disheveled or out of sorts.

The most obvious choice was the option that suggested someone entered the home after Mr. Davison had left, attacked Mrs. Davison as she sat down at her kitchen table to drink her coffee and read the newspaper, brutally assaulted her, raped her, and then left her unconscious, bleeding from her head, mouth, and vagina on the floor of her very own kitchen.

One can see how this thought terrified not only the citizenry of Texas City as the word got out, but also the Texas City Police Department itself. What type of person could ambush a 75-year-old grandmother, beat her mercilessly, violently rip off her undergarments, and sexually violate her? Then, after committing such an act, flee the scene and leave her there to slowly bleed to death. If the police could determine that Mrs. Davison was still breathing, surely the suspect could tell that she was still alive as well. Unfortunately, though, Mrs. Davison would not continue breathing for much longer.

One of the officers at the scene of the crime, Officer Deril Oliver, left The Davison Home after Police Chief Rankin DeWalt arrived and he proceeded to the Galveston County Memorial Hospital where Mrs. Davison had been taken. Amazingly, this hospital still stands until this very day, and it is still the most prominent hospital in Texas City. Albeit it has changed names several times.

Early in the history of Texas City there had been discussions amongst Galveston County doctors about the need for a hospital located on the mainland in Galveston County. Although some people argued that it was not a necessity, The Texas City Disaster of 1947 convinced residents that the area did in fact need its own hospital. In 1949, a $1 million bond was passed, and 13.5 acres were donated by the Maco Stewart Family of Galveston for the purpose of opening a facility on the mainland. The Galveston Memorial Hospital officially opened its doors at 7 a.m. on May 27, 1952.

If you were looking for this hospital today, you would not be able to find it under the name Galveston County Memorial Hospital. In 1976, the name was changed to the Memorial Hospital of Galveston, and it was changed again in 1984 and renamed the Mainland Center Hospital. In 1995, the hospital was acquired by Columbia/HCA Healthcare Inc. and was renamed Mainland Medical Center. In 1996, the name changed to Columbia Mainland Medical Center, but the name was changed back to Mainland Medical Center in 1999. Today, it is known as HCA Houston Healthcare Mainland. **(See Photo 1A at the end of this chapter.)**

Upon arriving at the hospital, Officer Oliver spoke with a neurosurgeon named Dr. C. Born, and with Dr. Eames. They reported that Mrs. Davison was still unconscious, she was in critical condition, and her skull was badly fractured. They also stated that Mrs. Davison possibly suffered brain damage from her wounds, however, they still needed to run more tests to be sure. Dr. Eames reported that there was severe damage to her vaginal area, but he was currently unable to determine to what extent.

While Mrs. Davison was still inside the examination room where the doctors were working diligently to stabilize her condition, Officer Oliver requested certain items from off her person that the police needed to assist with their investigation. He asked the doctors for the clothing that Mrs. Davison was wearing so that any evidence on it could be collected. Dr. Born complied with this request and he used a pair of scissors to cut the clothing off Mrs. Davison's unconscious frame.

Dr. Born cut off Mrs. Davison's red and white striped cotton house coat; he cut off her white gown, and he placed these items inside of a white sheet. He then removed the hairnet she was wearing and placed it inside of the white sheet as well. Then, he wrapped all of these items up together inside of the sheet and gave them to Officer Oliver.

Now, by today's standards, one might question the method used to package and transport these items, but it is important to remember that this crime occurred in 1970. Some methods which may seem crude to us now were widely accepted back then. Also, the idea of contaminating the evidence was not as fully developed back then as it is now. It is not my belief that Officer Oliver or Dr. Born were trying to corrupt any potential evidence. On the contrary. I believe they both saw placing these items inside of a white sheet as perfectly acceptable by the standards at the time.

After removing the clothing from off Mrs. Davison's body, the hospital staff covered her up in hospital garb and prepared her to be transferred from the examination room to the x-ray room. They determined that they needed to take some x-rays of her skull so that they could better assess the extent of her head injuries and determine a method of treatment. While in the x-ray room undergoing multiple tests, Mrs. Davison was under the constant care of both Dr. Born and Dr. Eames.

Then, after several hours of fighting for her life, Mrs. Ida Davison succumbed to her wounds and passed away. She was pronounced dead by Dr. Born at 12:00 noon on September 19, 1970, inside of the x-ray room. The crime had just escalated from breaking and entering and criminal assault to cold-blooded murder. The doctor informed Officer Oliver of the unfortunate turn of events, and the news of the death was quickly shared with Chief DeWalt and the rest of the Texas City Police Department. All officers were put on notice that they were now looking for a vicious murderer who was still at-large, roaming the streets of Texas City, possibly searching for more victims.

Officer Oliver knew that he needed to collect more evidence from the body of the recently deceased woman if they ever hoped to find and convict the killer. Part of their training instilled in every single officer the importance of gathering evidence. Even if the officer did not personally understand the relevance of the evidence they were gathering, they were explicitly trained to gather as much as possible. The reason for this was centered around the possibility of a future trial once the suspect was arrested and charged. The prosecutor would be dependent upon the evidence gathered by the cops who initially responded to the crime.

Officer Oliver scraped dried blood from the right hand of Mrs. Davison and placed the traces in an envelope furnished by the hospital. Her fingernails were also scraped and clipped and stored in a separate envelope which was tagged as evidence. It is important to note that in this modern era, DNA evidence is sometimes the most conclusive form of evidence which a prosecutor or defense attorney can present in court. DNA evidence can be used to either prove innocence or guilt. This was not the case in 1970, however. DNA was not used in courts in the United States until 1986, so the blood scrapings that were collected were not collected with the intention of extracting DNA. It was collected to compare blood types. But that will become more apparent later.

After this evidence was collected, Sgt. Joe Standley and the Galveston County deputy medical examiner arrived and conducted the necessary investigation which needs to be done whenever someone is murdered. Then, it was ordered that the body of Mrs. Davison be removed from

Galveston County Memorial Hospital and transported to the Medical Examiner's Office at John Sealy Hospital in Galveston, Tx. so that an autopsy could be conducted. According to the records, her body was removed from the hospital by Emkin-Linton Funeral Service.

By this time, the news of the crime had reached reporters from The Galveston Daily News, and they reached out to Police Chief Rankin DeWalt for comment. Chief DeWalt gave a statement to the reporters because at this time, he thought that getting the facts out to the public could assist the police in finding the culprit. This statement by Chief DeWalt became the infamous headline we mentioned earlier.

Texas City Woman, 75, Murdered!

Photo 1A

Photo Taken When The Hospital Was Named Galveston County Memorial Hospital

Chapter 6

The Investigation Leads Police To A Prime Suspect

As police searched high and low within the city limits, the body of Mrs. Ida Davison was transported to John Sealy Hospital in Galveston, Tx. It was here that her autopsy was conducted, and more details of the gruesome crime were discovered. The autopsy itself was conducted around 3:25 p.m. on the same day as the crime, September 19, 1970. It was performed by a doctor named Dr. Kurt Weiss. This doctor was the Assistant Medical Examiner of Galveston County, and he held this position since June 22, 1970.

Dr. Kurt Weiss studied medicine in Hamburg, Germany and his specialty was pathology. Pathology is a branch of medical science that is focused on the study and diagnosis of disease. Clinical pathology involves the examination of surgically removed organs, tissues (biopsy samples), bodily fluids, and, in some cases, the whole body (autopsy). So, given this background and level of education, he would have been considered the perfect person to conduct this autopsy and determine the particulars of what series of events the evidence pointed to.

Dr. Kurt Weiss determined that the official cause of death for Mrs. Ida Davison was a fractured skull and extensive brain damage which was the result of a severe blow with a blunt instrument. In his professional opinion, he is on record stating that the fracture to her skull could have been caused by a human fist. He also noted that there were contusions and abrasions on the right side of the victim's face and neck. He concluded that she had been struck multiple times, and it was possible that she had fallen from a seated position onto the floor.

He said that the blows to the head, face, and neck caused hemorrhaging that eventually led to the victim's death. He made it clear that no other possible cause of death was present. It was the fractured skull and the internal injuries it caused, that led to Mrs. Ida Davison's death. While performing the autopsy he noticed that those were not the only injuries she suffered.

Upon further examination, he determined that she also had extensive damage done to her vagina. So much so that there was bleeding inside of the vagina as well. He determined that the damage done to her vagina went about 5 to 6 inches deep and it was no doubt caused by the insertion of a foreign object. This foreign object, Dr. Kurt Weiss proclaimed, could have been a male penis. In fact, he stated that the damage to her vagina was almost certainly caused by the insertion of a male penis.

As more time passed, the picture of what took place inside of The Davison Home that morning became more and more clear. The information from the autopsy was transmitted to the Texas City Police Department, and this made the officers even more determined to find the culprit. They did not have anyone in custody at this time, but they did have some promising leads, and they had already come up with the name of a primary suspect. Lucky for them, this particular neighborhood was vigilant. They looked out for one another, and they did not hesitate to report suspicious activity. Had it not been for this propensity of the people living in this area to look out for one another, the murderer might have gotten away with this heinous violation of the elderly.

As the TCPD canvased the area and interviewed neighbors, it was learned that two 911 calls were made to that same area earlier that day prior to the murder. These two 911 calls were in reference to a suspicious person. The caller spoke of a young colored man appearing to be on drugs, walking up and down the block, and peeking in the window of a local business. In fact, two of the police officers who responded to the 911 call at The Davison Home had reported seeing this exact same suspicious person in the area mere minutes before the murder. At the time, however, they did not know that he was the suspicious character, nor did they know that in a few minutes Mrs. Ida Davison would be attacked inside of her home.

The first person to see the suspicious character was a 52-year-old woman named Sarah Parker. Mrs. Parker lived about a block away from The Davison Home at 216 3rd Ave N. According to her own report, she was up at around 6:50 that morning looking out of her window towards the home of a woman named Mrs. Carmen Reyes. Mrs. Reyes owned a business in the area called I-C Fish Market and Grocery, and Mrs. Parker was waiting to see Mrs. Reyes walking to open her store. Mrs. Parker said that she had run out of coffee, and she needed to walk to the I-C Fish Market and Grocery and purchase some before she had to go to work. **(See Photo 1A and 2A at the end of this chapter.)**

While she was looking out her window, she saw a young colored male run across the street in the middle of the 200 block of 3rd St N. The young man had run from east to west and into an alley. A few minutes later, at around 6:55 a.m., she saw Mrs. Reyes leave her home and begin walking toward her store. Knowing that she would be opening up around 7:00 a.m. once she arrived, Mrs. Parker left her home and began walking towards the store herself. The I-C Fish Market and Grocery was located in the same neighborhood at 202 3rd St. N.

At around 7:00 a.m., while walking to the store, Mrs. Parker says that she saw the same young colored man run back across the street and peek inside the window of the I-C Fish Market, apparently secretly watching Mrs. Reyes, who had just entered the building and was preparing to open up for the day. Thinking this was odd, she kept a close eye on the young man as she approached the store, and once she got closer, she recognized who he was. She reported that the young man was wearing goldish brown cut-off pants and a goldish brown undershirt.

Texas City is a small town today in 2025, and it was even smaller back in 1970. Almost everyone knew everyone. When asked for the name of the young man she saw, Mrs. Sarah Parker told police that the person she saw was a Texas City teen named Johnnie Avie. Johnnie was about 18 years old, and she said that she knew him by his nickname. Everyone called Johnnie, "Pie", and "Pie" was how she knew him.

"Pie." Mrs. Parker called out, once she got close enough to him to recognize who he was. "What do you have on your mind running around out here and peeking through the window of the Fish Market?"

Pie assured her that he didn't have anything on his mind, but she wasn't convinced. Pie had quite a reputation around Texas City, and he was always getting into something that would end up with him on the wrong side of the law. Mrs. Parker said she didn't have enough time to lecture him or investigate further because she had to go to work that morning, but she told him that whatever it was he had on his mind wasn't right and she told him that he should just leave the area and go home. Pie agreed to go home, and he walked off behind a house that sat next to the Fish Market.

Mrs. Parker also noticed that Pie was acting very strange and he had what she described as "a funny look in his eyes." Continuing on her journey, she made it to the store, went inside, exchanged pleasantries with Mrs. Reyes for a moment, and then purchased her coffee. When she left the store, she began walking north on 3rd St back toward her home. As she passed by the house that she saw Pie walk behind earlier, she turned around and was shocked to see that Johnnie Avie, aka Pie, was back outside the I-C Fish Market and Grocery peeking in through the window again.

It seemed to her as if he had simply hidden out while she conducted her business inside of the store and waited for her to leave. Then, as soon as she left the building, he went right back to stalking Mrs. Reyes. Mrs. Parker began to get a sinking feeling in the pit of her stomach, and she knew that she had to do something. Like I said, everyone in the neighborhood looked out for each other, and she could not in good conscious go back home without letting Mrs. Reyes know that she was seemingly being stalked by Johnnie Avie.

Mrs. Parker did the right thing. She promptly turned around and walked back to the store. Upon entering the building, she told Mrs. Reyes what she had seen and suggested that she call the police. The two women decided that if Pie was indeed plotting something sinister, if he saw the police riding around, he would abandon his plans and leave the area. Mrs. Reyes thanked Mrs. Parker for the advice and called the police and asked them to just ride by from time to time and check on her store.

Feeling thankful that her friend decided to call the police, Mrs. Parker returned to her home. Once there, she drank her coffee and prepared herself to go to work. She did not leave her house again until around 7:40 a.m. When she left her house to walk to work, she said that she saw Pie again walking east on 3rd Ave N in front of her house, and again she spoke to him. She says that she told him he should not have dropped out of school, and she suggested that he go back. Mrs. Parker was trying to give him some good advice about how to get his life back on track.

"Ok Mama Sarah." Pie replied, seeming to take the positive advice to heart, before continuing to walk east on 3rd Ave N.

After speaking with Pie, Mrs. Parker continued walking to her job. Presumably, her shift began at 8:00 a.m. At that time, she worked as a maid at Leon's Motel at 626 2nd Ave N. You should also note that if Pie were to walk east on 3rd Ave N in front of Mrs. Parker's house, it would lead him directly to The Davison Home.

Outside of law enforcement, the other person to see the primary suspect in the area prior to the murder was the aforementioned owner of the I-C Fish Market and Grocery, Carmen Reyes. Not only did she see the suspect in the area that morning, she is the one who called the police about him, not once, but twice. One can't help but to imagine that if the police had responded correctly to her two 911 calls, Mrs. Davison would not have died that day.

According to the official records, Mrs. Carmen Reyes was a 44-year-old woman who lived at 319 3ʳᵈ Ave N. She stayed half a block away from Mrs. Parker, and 1 ½ blocks away from The Davison Home. She reported to police that around 6:55 a.m. she left her home on foot, walking to work. As she walked, she claimed that she saw a colored male standing in the middle of the road slapping his legs. **(See Photo 3A at the end of this chapter.)**

As she got closer, the young man looked up and she recognized him as one of the Avie boys. She stated that he was wearing a pair of goldish brown cut-off shorts, a goldish brown undershirt, and a pair of sandals. As she got closer to him, Mrs. Reyes asked Johnnie Avie if the mosquitoes were biting him, and he responded by saying they were. After this brief interaction, she continued on to her store and went through the necessary process to open the store for business.

According to Mrs. Reyes, she opened the store around 7:00 a.m., and one of her first customers, if not her very first customer, was none other than the aforementioned Mrs. Sarah Parker. Now remember, these are two independent witness accounts telling the exact same story about what happened that morning.

Mrs. Reyes told police that when Mrs. Parker came in, she bought coffee and left. Then, she returned to the store and told her about the suspicious behavior of Johnnie Avie peeking in through the window. She also said that Mrs. Parker warned her that Avie appeared to be up to no good, and she suggested that Mrs. Reyes call the police. Heeding the warning, Mrs. Reyes said that she locked her doors after Mrs. Parker left, and she would only open the door for legitimate customers.

Alerted to the danger, Mrs. Reyes began watching her windows more intensely. She said that after Mrs. Parker left, she noticed Avie peeking in through her store windows and coming up to the door several times and trying to open it. As she looked on from a safe distance, she echoed the sentiment of Mrs. Parker and said that Avie had a strange look in his eyes. She even went further to say that he looked either drunk or doped up.

Mrs. Reyes was made so uncomfortable by the actions of Johnnie Avie, and the warnings of Mrs. Sarah Parker, that she decided to make a 911 call to the Texas City Police Department. According to the official records, at 7:12 a.m., Mrs. Carmen Reyes placed a call to the Texas City Police Department and reported that there was a suspicious boy lurking around the neighborhood. She wasn't reporting a specific crime, but she did ask that the police drive by her business periodically to deter any would-be criminals from committing any criminal acts.

Below is a copy of the actual police report documenting the 911 call that Mrs. Carmen Reyes made at 7:12 a.m. on the morning of the murder.

Police Department

COMPLAINT NO. 113??   DATE 9-19-70   TIME 0712

NAME Manager Fishmarket   PHONE

ADDRESS 202 3rd. St. N,

REPORTS Sup. Boy.

DISP. Reno

OFFICER ASSIGNED 752-Cole

OFFICER REPORT

DATE 9-19-70   OFFICER

Murder File: Police Report Of 911 Call Made By Mrs. Carmen Reyes

The police responded to this call, and Officer Cole was dispatched to the area to drive by and check on the store. Between 7:12 a.m. and 7:55 a.m., Johnnie Avie came back to the store several more times. Each time he came, he checked the door to see if it was still locked, and he peeked in through the window. We can't be sure of exactly what he was doing during this time, but we know for a fact that he was wandering around in the area the entire time. It is possible that he peeked into the window of several homes, and not seeing anything that caught his attention, continued to make his way back to the store.

One can only imagine what would have happened to Mrs. Carmen Reyes that morning if she had not received a warning from Mrs. Sarah Parker and locked her door. Perhaps this book would be about her instead of being about Mrs. Ida Davison.

At 7:55 a.m., Mrs. Reyes could not take the suspicious actions of Avie any longer and she made a second 911 call to the Texas City Police Department. This time, instead of asking officers to ride around in the area, she specifically asked to speak with an officer face to face. She had become convinced that Avie was up to no good and she was beginning to get afraid.

Below is a copy of the actual police report documenting the 911 call that Mrs. Carmen Reyes made at 7:55 a.m. on the morning of the murder.

Murder File: Police Report Of 911 Call Made By Mrs. Carmen Reyes

The dispatch officer contacted Officer Gilmore and instructed him to go to the I-C Fish Market and Grocery to speak with Mrs. Reyes. When he arrived, Mrs. Reyes told Officer Gilmore everything that had taken place that morning, and she let him know that she did not feel safe with Avie lurking around in the neighborhood. When she gave the officer the description of the suspicious young man, Officer Gilmore realized that he saw the suspect walking in the 200 block of 3rd Ave N when he was driving to the store. He is on record as saying while he was in route he saw a tall colored male wearing a brown undershirt and short gold-colored pants.

10 minutes before the second 911 call, which was made at 7:55 a.m., another officer claimed to have seen Johnnie Avie in the area. At 7:45 a.m., Officer George Eden stated that while he was doing his routine patrol, he saw Johnnie Avie walking south in the 200 block of 3rd St N. This was prior to the second 911 call, so officer Eden had no reason to pull Avie over and detain him. Officer Eden knew Avie from several previous arrests, so we can be sure that he was able to positively identify the young man he saw, just like Mrs. Parker and Mrs. Reyes did.

With these four eyewitnesses adding more pieces to the puzzle, the overall picture became even more clear. The police were able to create a more detailed timeline, and they were now able to name a suspect. All available officers were put on notice to be on the lookout for an 18-year-old black male named Johnnie Avie, aka Pie. The description associated with the suspect was that he was a tall black male, approximately 6 '5, and he was last seen wearing a goldish brown shirt, goldish brown cut off shorts, and a pair of sandals.

If Avie turned out to indeed be the murderer, the police now had a timeline of events that led up to the murder. Let's look at this timeline in a more linear fashion so that you can understand the series of events better.

6:50 a.m. – Mrs. Sarah Parker sees Avie run across the street in the 200 block of 3rd St N while waiting for Mrs. Carmen Reyes to open her store.

6:55 a.m. – Mrs. Carmen Reyes leaves her home and sees Avie in the middle of the street while walking to work. She speaks to him and continues on.

7:00 a.m. – Mrs. Sarah Parker leaves her house to walk to the store and sees Avie peeking in the window of the I-C Fish Market and Grocery, watching Mrs. Reyes. Getting closer she recognizes Avie and speaks briefly with him.

7:05 a.m. – Mrs. Parker leaves the store and again sees Avie peeking in through the window, then goes back and suggests that Mrs. Reyes call the police.

7:05 a.m. – 7:12 a.m. – Avie continues to come back to the store checking the door and peeking in through the window.

7:12 a.m. – Mrs. Reyes calls the police and reports a suspicious boy lurking around her store. Officer Cole is assigned.

7:40 a.m. – Mrs. Parker leaves her home headed to work, sees Avie again, and has a short conversation with him.

7:45 a.m. – Officer Eden sees Avie walking south in the 200 block of 3rd St. N while on his routine patrol.

7:55 a.m. – Mrs Reyes, after seeing Avie peeking in her store window several more times, makes another 911 call, and requests an officer to come and speak with her directly.

7:55 a.m. – 8:00 a.m. – Officer Gilmore sees Avie walking in the 200 block of 3rd Ave. N while enroute to the I-C Fish Market and Grocery.

Shortly after this last sighting of Johnnie Avie, the murderer would be entering through the front door of The Davison Home, catching Mrs. Ida off guard in her kitchen reading the newspaper, violently attacking her, beating her, raping her, and then leaving her for dead as they fled the scene. Considering these facts, it's no doubt why Johnnie Avie became the prime suspect in this case. There were only two questions.

Was he the actual murderer?

Where was he now?

Photo 1A

THE STATE OF TEXAS
COUNTY OF GALVESTON .

Before me, the undersigned authority in and for said county and state, on this the 20th

day of ... September ...... A. D. 19. 70 , personally appeared . Mrs. Sarah Parker ....
who after being by me duly sworn, deposes and says:

My name is Sarah Herman Parker. I am 47 years old and reside at 216 3rd Ave N.,
Texas City, Texas. I am employed as a Maid at Leona Motel, 626 2nd Ave N., in
Texas City.

At approximately 6:50 A.M., yesterday, September 19, I was looking out the window
of my house watching for Mrs. Reyes, at the 10 Fish Market to open the store as I
was out of coffee. As I was watching I saw a young colored male run across the
street in the middle of the block of the 200 Block of 3rd St N. He came from the
east side of the street and I saw him run into the alley on the west side of the
street. A few minutes later I saw Mrs. Reyes walking toward her store on 3rd St
in the 200 Block. I then left my house and started walking to the store. As I
turned the corner onto 3rd St I saw the same boy run back across the street and
saw him peeking in the window of the store. As I got close to him I recognized
him as Johnny Avie, who I call "Pie." Her was wearing a pair of goldish brown
cut-off pants, and a goldish brown undershirt. I asked him what he had on his
mind and told him that whatever it was it wasn't right. He said he didn't have
nothing on his mind and I told him then he better go home. He said O.K. and I
saw him go behind the house located next to the store. I noticed when I was talking
to him that he acted strange and he had a funny look in his eyes. I then went
into the store and got my coffee. When I left the store I started walking north
on 3rd St. When I got past the house next to the Store I turned around and saw
"Pie" in front of the store looking in the window again. I then went back to the
store and told Mrs. Reyes to lock her doors and to call the Police. I then went
home. Approximately 20 minutes later I left my house to go to work. As I came
at the door I saw "Pie" walking east on 3rd Ave N. in front of my house. It .

Subscribed and sworn to before me, the undersigned authority, on this the .... day of
.... 19 70
WITNESS: ....
WITNESS: ....
(Notary Public in and for Galveston County, Texas

Murder File: Sarah Parker's Statement To Police Pg 1

99

Photo 2A

THE STATE OF TEXAS
COUNTY OF GALVESTON

Before me, the undersigned authority in and for said county and state, on this the _____

day of _____ A. D. 19____, personally appeared _____,
who after being by me duly sworn, deposes and says:

would have been about 20 minutes to 8 when I left the house. I talked to "Pie"
again and asked him why he had dropped out of school and told he ought to go back.
He said "O.K., Mama Sarah", and then continued walking east on 3rd Ave N. I then
went on to work.

Subscribed and sworn to before me, the undersigned authority, on this the 20th day of
September 19 71.

WITNESS: _____
WITNESS: _____

Notary Public in and for Galveston County, Texas
My Commission Expires 6-7-71

1.58 P.m. 9-20-70

Murder File: Sarah Parker's Statement To Police Pg 2

Photo 3A

THE STATE OF TEXAS
COUNTY OF GALVESTON

Before me, the undersigned authority in and for said county and state, on this the   20th

day of September   A. D. 19 70 , personally appeared Mrs. Carmen Rivera Reyes   .
who after being by me duly sworn, deposes and says:

My name is Carmen Rivera Reyes. I am 44 years old and reside at 319 3rd Avenue

North, Texas City, Texas. I am the owner and operator of the IC Fish Market &

Grocery, which is located at 202 3rd Street N., Texas City.

At approximately 6:55 A.M., yesterday, September 19, I left my house to walk

to the Store. I walked east on 3rd Ave N., and turned south on 3rd St N. As I

turned the corner I saw a colored male in approximately the middle of the block,

bending over slapping at his legs. As I got close to him he looked up and I

recognized him as one of the Avie boys. He was wearing a pair of goldish brown

cut-off pants, a goldish brown undershirt and a pair of sandels. As I passed him

I spoke to him and asked him if the mosquitoes were biting him. He said "yes"

and I went on to the store. After I opened the store a customer, Mrs. Sarah

Parker, who lives on 3rd St N., came in, bought some coffee, and told me to be

careful because she said that after I went into the store the boy I had spoken

to had come over to the store and peeked in the window and then run back across

the street. After I let Mrs. Parker out I locked the door and would only open

it to let customers in. Several times I saw the Avie boy come up to the door

and try to open it and then leave. After he had come to the door several times

I looked at him and noticed that his eyes looked strange and thought he was

either drunk or doped up. I then called the Police and asked them to keep a

check on my store. The boy came back to the store several more times and tried

the door and at about 8:00 A.M. I decided to call the Police again. I did'nt

see the boy anymore after calling the Police.

Mrs Carmen Rivera Reyes

Subscribed and sworn to before me, the undersigned authority, on this the   20 th   day of

September   1970   J. D. Schraeder

WITNESS: I.C. Reyes   Notary Public in and for Galveston County, Texas

WITNESS: William R Henry   My Commission Expires

6 - 1 - 71

12:10 PM   9 20 70

Murder File: Carmen Reyes Statement To Police

Chapter 7

Johnnie Avie Gets Arrested

Police Chief Rankin DeWalt had given all Texas City Police Officers explicit instructions that no one could rest until the person who murdered Mrs. Ida Davison was captured, so all available units were on the hunt for their prime suspect, 18-year-old Johnnie Avie. Many of the officers on the police force knew of Avie personally because of his past criminal history, but some of them only knew his description. However, a 6'5 young black male wearing a goldish brown shirt and gold-colored shorts would definitely stand out in a crowd. It was only a matter of time before he was spotted and arrested.

But who exactly was Johnnie Avie? **(See Photo 1A at the end of this chapter.)**

Johnnie Avie was born on August 20, 1952, in the Ft. Hood Texas military base. His father was a man named Jeffery Avie, and his mother was named Louise Avie. Johnnie attended Texas City Public Schools, and growing up, he loved playing basketball, baseball, and he had a fondness for antique and flea markets browsing and shopping. His parents did the best they could at raising him, but for some reason, at an early age, Johnnie began ending up on the wrong side of the law, and it was this propensity for criminal behavior that grew to dominate his public persona.

Johnnie Avie had several run-ins with the law prior to the murder of Mrs. Ida Davison even though he was only 18 at the time at the time the crime was committed. He began running afoul of the law at a very early age, and he was known to hang out in questionable places with questionable people and engage in criminal activities. According to his official arrest record, Johnnie Avie was arrested at least 13 times prior to the murder of Mrs. Ida. His first crime on record took place when he was only 14 years old. After this first arrest, Avie continued break to law and get arrested. In fact, Avie was arrested again just 8 days before the murder took place.

On July 5, 1967, when Avie was only 14 years old, he was arrested for the first time by TCPD Officers Boydson and Freeman. He was charged with Burglary, Purse Snatching, and Theft.

On March 5, 1968, when Avie was 15 years old, he was arrested by TCPD Officer Eden for Theft and Burglary.

On March 9, 1968, 4 days after his prior arrest, Avie was arrested again by TCPD Officer Steele for Disturbing the Peace.

On November 2, 1968, TCPD Officer Eden arrested Avie again for the charge of Robbery by Assault. He was only 16 years old.

On April 4, 1969, when Avie was only 16 years old, he was again arrested for Disturbing the Peace by TCPD Officer Gross.

On July 29, 1969, TCPD Officer Eden arrested Avie for a third time. This time, Avie was charged again with Assault and Robbery.

On January 24, 1970, at 17 years old, Avie was arrested by TCPD Officer Scott for Intoxication and Curfew Violation.

One would think that after so many back-to-back arrests between the ages of 14 and 17, Johnnie Avie, aka Pie, would've reconsidered a life of crime, but that is not the case. In fact, he continued on with the same pattern of behavior. It would appear that he did not mind breaking the law, and even after being charged with a particular crime, he had a propensity to commit that exact same criminal act again.

On February 20, 1970, Avie was arrested again for Assault by TCPD Officer Cohen.

On April 23, 1970, Avie was arrested by TCPD Officer Eden for Gaming.

On the official records that I obtained, his next 3 arrests have the dates somewhat cut off. I know the day and year of the offense, but I do not know which month they occurred in. However, we can tell for certain that they occurred between May 21, 1970, and September 7, 1970.

On the 21st of one of those months, Avie was arrested by TCPD Officer Ball for Indecent Exposure.

On the 12th of one of those months, Avie was arrested by TCPD Officer Eden for Disorderly Conduct.

On the 7th of one of those months, Avie was arrested by TCPD Officer Fleming for Intoxication.

On September 11, 1970, when Avie was 18 years old, he was arrested by TCPD Officers Gross and Lawrence for Consumption of Alcohol at an Athletic Contest.

This last arrest, which took place on the 11th of September, was a mere 8 days prior to the September 19th murder. **(See Photo 2A at the end of this chapter.)** When we read over Avie's exhaustive criminal record between the ages of 14 and 18, we get the picture painted for us of a troubled youth who terrorized the streets of Texas City, Tx. We can also see a pattern of behavior that the police department no doubt saw as well. Johnnie Avie had no problem robbing and stealing and if his victim objected to his crimes, he was more than willing to assault them.

We can see that Avie also was arrested multiple times for being intoxicated, disturbing the peace, and disorderly conduct. All of this was considered by the TCPD when they analyzed the available evidence in search of a subject. It was also interesting that Mrs. Sarah Parker and Mrs. Carmen Reyes claimed that the morning of the murder, Johnnie Avie had a strange look in his eyes as if he was high when they saw him.

There is one more arrest on his record that stood out under the current circumstances. On one occasion we see that Officer Ball arrested Avie for Indecent Exposure. Although we do not know the specifics of this case, we can infer what might have happened based on the legal definition of this crime and what it implies.

Indecent Exposure - The act of intentionally exposing one's private body parts in a way that is offensive, or which goes against accepted behavior, in a public place.

But what exactly is Indecent Exposure? While some people believe they can do nearly anything they want in the name of "freedom of expression," it is against the law to expose certain private body parts in a place where the public can see it. Areas of the body that cannot be legally exposed or shown in public include genitals, inner buttocks, and female nipples. The law does not require that any person actually sees the exposure, but considers whether the perpetrator has, or should have, a reasonable belief that the act could be viewed by others.

From this legal definition and explanation, we can see that Avie could've caught this charge by actually exposing himself to someone in public or exposing himself in public in a manner which caused someone else to believe that his genitals could be seen by others. Perhaps he was simply urinating in public, or perhaps he was showing off his manhood to some unsuspecting and unparticipating victim. At any rate, a rap sheet like his would have put all cops on high alert as they searched for Avie under the suspicion that he was the one who broke into The Davison Home, attacked Mrs. Ida Davison, and violently raped her.

It took approximately 7 ½ hours of hardcore police work to locate and arrest their suspect. At 5:17 p.m., the same day that the crime was committed, TCPD Officers Fred Monroe and George Eden were walking into the Texas City Police Station with the biggest arrest of their careers. The two officers happened to come across Avie walking at the intersection of 6ᵗʰ St and 2 Ave S. Officer Eden had arrested Avie about 5 times prior to this new arrest, so it almost seemed fitting that he was the one to hunt him down and bring him to justice on this new offense. From all of his previous encounters with Avie, he no doubt had some extra insight into the areas that Avie frequented, as well as the people he hung out with that could give him information pertaining to Avie's whereabouts.

Once Johnnie Avie was in custody, the TCPD immediately proceeded to collect any evidence which may have been on his person, and they also began to piece together a timeline of events to account for his whereabouts when the murder occurred and immediately after. They already knew that the last person who reported seeing Avie was Officer Gilmore. Officer Gilmore stated that at around 7:55 a.m., when he was enroute to the I-C Fish Market and Grocery to speak with Mrs. Carmen Reyes, he saw Avie walking south in the 200 block of 3ʳᵈ St N. This sighting definitively placed Avie about a block away from The Davison Home 10 mins after Mr. Don Davison left his wife alone that fateful morning.

News of the arrest was initially withheld from the public. The police needed time to acquire evidence and question the suspect before they could release news to the press that they had indeed arrested their number one suspect. Subsequently, the day after the arrest, the story appeared in the Galveston Daily News stating that the police were still searching for the suspect. However, when the general public were reading this statement by Police Chief Rankin DeWalt, Johnnie Avie was already in police custody, and the investigation was in full swing.

The day after the murder, September 20, 1970, the police department had formally charged Avie with the murder, and so they felt comfortable releasing the new facts to the press. They contacted the Galveston Daily News once more, and the staff writer who wrote the initial piece about the murder was called upon to jump back in the proverbial saddle and write a new piece detailing the arrest of the prime suspect. The police couldn't tell him all of the evidence they had on Avie, but they gave him enough information for yet another explosive article.

On September 21, 1970, staff writer Jerry Cooper wrote the second most impactful story of his career, and it reverberated through Texas City harder than his initial story about the murder itself. Again, Texas City was a small town back then and many people in both the white and black communities knew who Johnnie Avie was. Also, the head editor for the paper decided to print the story on the front page. It was therefore impossible to miss.

Man Arrested
On Murder Rap

By JERRY COOPER
NEWS STAFF WRITER

TEXAS CITY — An 18 year - old former Texas City youth has been charged with murder with malice in connection with the beating death of prominent Texas Citian, Mrs. Don C. (Ida) Davison, Saturday morning.

Johnny Avie, current address given as 10 East Oleander Homes, Galveston, was picked up by Texas City police officers George Eden and Fred Monroe at the intersection of 6th Street and 2nd Ave. South at 5:17 p.m. Saturday and formally charged before Justice of the Peace T. A. Bishop at 10:15 p.m. that day.

Avie was reportedly seen by police officers near the 100 3rd Ave. North Davison home where the beating allegedly took place. A reliable source reported that the suspect gave police a confession, but Texas City Police Chief Rankin DeWalt declined to comment on the matter.

An autopsy revealed that Mrs. Davison died from a broken skull as a result of being beaten with a blunt instrument. Dr. Kurt G. Weiss, medical examiner, said that she had also been criminally assaulted prior to her death.

DeWalt said the investigation into the slaying is continuing.

He said that a preliminary hearing for Avie will likely be held within the next two weeks and "we're ready any time now."

DeWalt also declined to comment on evidence in the case, but the clothing that Avie was reportedly wearing at the time of his arrest was stained with what appeared to be blood.

The suspect was being held in the Texas City jail without bond Sunday night.

Galveston Daily News September 21, 1970

Man Arrested On Murder Rap

***Texas City** – An 18-year-old former Texas City youth has been charged with murder with malice in connection with the beating death of prominent Texas Citian, Mrs. Don C. (Ida) Davison, Saturday morning.*

Johnnie Avie, current address given as 10 East Oleander Homes, Galveston, was picked up by Texas City police officers George Eden and Fred Monroe at the intersection of 6th Street and 2nd Ave. South at 5:17 p.m.

110

Saturday and formally charged before Justice of the Peace T. A. Bishop at 10:15 p.m. that day.

Avie was reportedly seen by police officers near the 109 3ʳᵈ Ave. North Davison Home where the beating allegedly took place. A reliable source reported that the suspect gave police a confession, but Texas City Police Chief Rankin DeWalt declined to comment on the matter.

An autopsy revealed that Mrs. Davison died from a broken skull as a result of being beaten with a blunt instrument. Dr. Kurt G. Weiss, medical examiner, said that she had also been criminally assaulted prior to her death.

DeWalt said the investigation into the slaying is continuing.

He said that a preliminary hearing for Avie will likely be held within the next two weeks and "we're ready any time now."

DeWalt also declined to comment on evidence in the case, but the clothing that Avie was reportedly wearing at the time of his arrest was stained with what appeared to be blood.

The suspect was being held in Texas City jail without bond Sunday night.

According to the official records, we can piece together a loose timeline of events that Avie engaged in after the crime at The Davison Home was discovered. For the moment, we will discuss what he did and where he went without explicitly claiming that he committed the crime. We will examine more details about the crime itself later. After being spotted by law enforcement a block away from the scene of the crime, Johnnie Avie walked over to 109 1ˢᵗ Ave N to a friend's house. This friend was a man named Johnny McDaniel, and Avie claims that when he got there he went to sleep.

We do not know exactly what time he made it to Johnny McDaniel's house, but we do know that after going to sleep there, Avie woke up around 11:00 a.m. Then, he left Johnny McDaniel's house and made his way over to Johnson Pool Hall. What he did while there and who he spoke to is a mystery, but one could assume that he shot pool and had a few drinks while hanging out with friends. He hung out at the pool hall until around 1:00 p.m., and then he exited the building. When he stepped outside, he ran into another group of young men that he knew, walking down the street.

One of the young men he ran into after leaving the pool hall, 17-year-old Bruce Nathaniel Montgomery, voluntarily came forward on September 24ᵗʰ and gave the police a statement detailing his interactions with Avie after he learned that Avie was arrested for the murder of Mrs. Ida. **(See Photo 3A at the end of this chapter.)** He said that when Avie came out of the pool hall he began walking with him and his small group of friends towards the old Booker T. Washington school. The young men had plans on going there to join a dice game. Reaching the old school building, they did indeed find a dice game underway, and they joined the game.

According to Bruce, they all shot dice for a while and then they left the old Booker T. Washington school walking back towards his house. At some point, he claims that Johnnie Avie said that he could not walk in the direction that they were walking in because the police were looking for him. It is interesting to note that if the group were walking from the school towards Bruce's house, the group would've been walking closer towards The Davison Home. Bruce said that Avie never explained exactly why the police were looking for him, and no one pressed him for more information. I suspect Avie had so many run-ins with the law that it came as no surprise to them to hear that he thought the TCPD was looking for him.

Bruce claims that him and three other young men separated from Avie around 2:30 p.m., and he did not see him anymore that day. He also told law enforcement that when he saw the suspect, Avie was wearing a brown nylon shirt, brown short pants, and sandals. This description was in line with the description of what all other witnesses saw Avie wearing that day.

Less than 3 hours after separating from Bruce's group, Avie would be getting picked up by the TCPD and taken into custody. The initial charge they picked him up on was an old traffic violation, but they took the opportunity to question him about the murder. As stated earlier, Avie was arrested and brought to the jail at 5:17 p.m. He was picked up at the intersection of 6th St and 2nd Ave S, a short 4 ½ blocks away from the scene of the crime.

Perhaps Avie couldn't get a ride back to Galveston, but one is left to wonder why he stayed so close to the scene of the crime for so many hours after the murder.

Photo 1A

Picture Of Johnnie Avie Taken While In Prison

Photo 2A

The following is a transcript of the record, including the most recently reported data and arrests, as shown in the Identification Bureau, Police Dept. Texas City, Texas, concerning our number:

8 8 1 1

FBI No.
DPS No.
FPC: 6 1 A2a 6
      1 tA2a

Johnnie (nmn) AVIE
M/M - DOB 8/20/1952

Date	Arr. No.	Officers	Charge	Case No.	Disposition
7/5/67	44053	Boydson-Freeman	Burg; purse snatching & Inv.Thefts (2 burgs. 5 thfts)	A-31461	Rel.to parents & J/O
3/5/68	45555	Eden	Theft & Inv.Burg.	A-34390	Rel.to J/O & Parents
3/9/68	45583	Steele	Dist. Peace	A-34460	Trans. Co. Jail
112/68	46993	Eden	Inv.Robbery by Assault	A-37731	Rel.to father 11/6/68 to see Juv.Off.Green
4/4/69	47880	Gross	Dist.Peace	A-39846	$25.00 fine, Rel.
7/29'69	48577	Eden	Inv.Aslt.& Robbery	A-41341	Rel.to see J/O Green
1/24/70	49719	Scott	Intox. & Curfew Viol.	A-43802	Rel. $40.00 Fine
2/20/70	49884	Cohen	Simp. Aslt. & Shplt.	A-44139	Rel. $250.00 J.P. Bond
4-3-70	50319	Eden	Gaming	A-45077	Rel. $25.00 Fine
-21-70	50494	Ball	Indecent Exposure	A-45457	Rel. $25.00 Fine
-17-70	50845	Eden	Disorderly Conduct	No Report	Rel. $15.00 Fine
4-7-70	51224	Fleming	Intoxication	A-47213	Rel. $25.00 Fine
9/11/70	51241	Gross-Lawrence	Consu. Alchol at Atheletic Contest	A-47260	Rel. to pay $75.00

Murder File: Johnnie Avie's Criminal Record

114

Photo 3A

Before me, the undersigned authority in and for said county and state, on this the **JULY 21** day of SEPTEMBER A. D. 19 70 , personally appeared BRUCE NATHANIEL MONTGOMERY . who after being by me duly sworn, deposes and says:

MY NAME IS BRUCE NATHANIEL MONTGOMERY, I AM 17 YEARS OLD AND LIVE AT 421-2nd AVENUE

SOUTH, TEXAS CITY, TEXAS.

AT ABOUT 1:00 PM ON SATURDAY THE 19th DAY OF SEPTEMBER 1970 I WAS WALKING WITH SOME

MORE GUYS PAST JOHNSONS POOL HALL WHEN JOHNNIE AVIE CAME OUT OF THE POOL HALL AND ASKED

US WHERE WE WERE GOING. I TOLD HIM WE WERE GOING TO THE OLD BOOKER T SCHOOL. JOHNNIE

START D WALKING WITH US AND WHEN WE GOT TO THE SCHOOL WE STARTED SHOOTING DICE. SOME

MORE GUYS CAME UP AND GOT INTO THE GAME BUT I DIDN'T PAY ANY ATTENTION XXXXX WHO THEY

WERE. WE PLAIN PLAYED FOR ABOUT AN HOUR AND THEN LEFT. JOHNNIE, MYSELF AND THE OTHER

THREE GUYS STARTED WALKING BACK TOWARD MY HOUSE WHEN I HEARD JOHNNIE SAY HE HAD BETTER

GO THE OTHER WAY BECAUSE THE LAW WAS LOOKING FOR HIM. HE DIDN'T SAY ANY BUT TOOK OFF IN

THE OPESITE DIRECTION FROM ME. I HAVN'T SEEN HIM SINCE.

JOHNNIE WAS WEARING A BROWN NYLON SHIRT, BROWN SHORT PANTS AND SANDLES.

WE SEPERATED ABOUT 2:30 PM

Nathaniel Montgomery

Subscribed and sworn to before me, the undersigned authority, on this the 24th day of
September 19 70 *L. Schroeder*
Notary Public in and for Galveston County, Texas
My Commission Expires
6-1-71

70   1705   9-24-70

Murder File: Bruce Montgomery Statement To Police

Chapter 8

Johnnie Avie Confesses To The Crime While In Police Custody

When Johnnie Avie was brought into the Texas City Police Station, the news of his arrest spread like wildfire throughout the entire department. Virtually all officers, from the Chief of Police to the officers working dispatch, were alerted to his capture. He wasn't immediately charged with the murder, though. Instead, he was arrested and taken into custody over some previous traffic violations. Initially he was only a person of interest in the murder of Mrs. Ida Davison. The police knew that since they had no witnesses to the crime itself, they needed some pretty concrete evidence before he could be formally charged.

The arresting officers noticed that Avie was still wearing the same clothes he was wearing that morning, and if he had in fact committed the crime, those would have been the same clothes he was wearing when he murdered Mrs. Ida. As they processed Avie into the jail, they made him remove his clothing in exchange for his jailhouse garb, and they found a total of about $4.50 in his possession. Officers took note that his shirt had what appeared to be blood spots on it, and so his shirt went directly into evidence. Also, when they took possession of his shorts and underwear, a large amount of blood was found on the front of both of them. This seemed to be in line with the suspicion that Mrs. Ida was both beaten and raped by her killer. Because of this, his shorts and underwear were placed into evidence as well.

After taking his clothes and sandals, the items were tagged as evidence and sent immediately over to the ID department so that they could be inspected further. This inspection confirmed what the officers suspected. The shirt, shorts, and cotton underwear of Avie indeed had blood on them. At this point one can only imagine what was going through Johnnie Avie's mind, but he must have felt the walls closing in on him. And the police, we can be sure that they were becoming more and more confident that they had their man.

Johnnie Avie sat inside of his cell with nothing but his thoughts for about a little over an hour before the police would speak to him again. At 6:30 p.m., September 19, 1970, Judge Ted Bishop arrived at the jail after being summoned by the police. The Judge gave Avie his statutory warning and advised him of his rights. They let him know that he did not have to answer any questions, he had a right to an attorney, and they informed him that anything he said could be used against him in the court of law.

At 6:35 p.m., Avie stated that he understood what his rights were, and he signed a waiver saying he understood his rights. At that point Avie was interrogated by the police. According to the official records, it appears that Officer Oliver conducted this first interview of the suspect. Officer Oliver was one of the first officers to arrive at the scene of the crime, and he was the same officer who went to the hospital and was there when Mrs. Ida passed away.

WAIVER-OF-RIGHTS FORM

On the _19th_ day of _September_ , 19_20_

David Olivas _____ advised
(Officer)

Johnny Avie _____ that he did not have to
(Subject)
tell him anything; that anything he did tell him might be used in evidence
against him in a court of law; that he had a right to an attorney; that he had
a right to have the attorney present while the officer was talking to him or
questioning him; that he did not have to say anything to the officer until his
attorney or lawyer was present; that if he talked to the officers he could terminate or stop talking to the officers any time he wanted to and that any time
he desired, an attorney would be called to assist him and no questions would
be asked him until the attorney arrived.

(signature) _____
(Signature of subject)

I, _David Olivas_ _____ , a member of the
Sugar City Police Dept _____ on the _19_ day of
September , 19_20_ , administered the foregoing warning to
Johnny Avie _____ before commencing an inter-
(Subject)
view with him.

David Olivas _____
(Signature of officer)

(If the subject refuses to sign this waiver, the officer should so note)

_1835   9-19-20_

Murder File: Johnnie Avie Waiver Of Rights Form

When asked about the murder, Avie outright denied
any involvement in the murder, and he even denied having
knowledge of it. The police thought that he was lying, but no
matter how hard they pressed him, Avie was remaining tight
lipped about any involvement he may have had. You have to

119

remember that Johnnie Avie was only 18 years old at the time, but he was no stranger to going foul of the law. He had been arrested, questioned, and locked inside of a cell plenty of times within the past four years. He no doubt thought that if he just denied committing the murder, he would never go down for it.

At this point Avie was taken back to his cell and the police continued to collect evidence and build their case. Between 6:35 p.m., and 8:40 p.m., we are not sure of exactly what took place inside of the jail, but at 8:40 p.m., Avie decided to give the police another statement which the police stated he gave voluntarily. This new statement was a partial confession to the crime he was being investigated for. Long after the arrest, several people who were watching this case unfold, wondered if the police had somehow coerced Avie into giving another statement, but there is no evidence available to us to corroborate this suspicion.

Perhaps it was simply the racial tension which existed in America in 1970 that led to various conspiracy theories. Headlines of a young black male violently beating, raping, and murdering an elderly white woman were no doubt reminiscent of the days when members of the black community were lynched and hung for simply looking directly at a white woman whether they actually committed a crime or not. Some people no doubt wondered if Avie was threatened or even beaten by police into making another statement which would incriminate himself.

However, as I stated earlier, I have come across no evidence to substantiate such a claim. As it stands, for whatever reason, Avie did in fact make this new statement voluntarily. Perhaps he was feeling guilty and wanted to clear his conscious. Perhaps he knew that the evidence would prove he had entered The Davison Home, and he wanted to manipulate the narrative. After all, going down for burglary was far better than going down for murder and rape. Whatever the reason was, at 8:40 p.m., on the same day the murder occurred, Johnnie Avie gave the following damning statement to the police.

My name is JOHNNY AVIE . I live at #10 E Olender Homes GALVESTON, GALVESTON TEXAS WITH MY MOTHER AND FATHER. I AM 18 YEARS OLD AND WORK ON CONSTRUCTION.

AT ABOUT 8:00 AM THIS MORNING, SATURDAY THE 19TH DAY OF SEPTEMBER 1970 I WENT TO THE OLD GREEN CASTLE ON THIRD AVENUE NORTH. I WENT THERE FOR THE PURPOSE OF STEALING SOME MONEY FROM THE PEOPLE THAT LIVE THERE. I KNOW THE PEOPLE BUT CAN NOT REMEMBER THEIR NAME. I FIRST WENT AROUND THE HOUSE AND LOOKED THROUGH THE WINDOWS BUT DID NOT SEE ANYONE. I NOTICED THE FRONT DOOR WAS OPEN SO I WENT INSIDE AND WENT TO THE KITCHEN. I FIRST NOTICED THE LADY THAT LIVES THERE WAS LYING IN THE KITCHEN FLOOR AND WAS BLEEDING FROM THE MOUTH. THERE WAS A LOT OF BLOOD ON THE FLOOR UNDER HER.

I FIRST WENT TO THE REFRIGERATOR AND OPENED IT UP AND LOOKED INSIDE AND THEN WENT UP STAIRS TO ONE OF THE BED ROOMS AND LOOKED AROUND FOR SOME MONEY. AFTER AWHILE I GOT SCARED AND STARTED RUNNING. I RAN OUT THE FRONT DOOR AND WENT TO MR JOHNNY McDANIELD HOUSE ON FIRST AVE NORTH.

THE CLOTHING AND SHOES THAT I WAS WEARING WHEN THE POLICE PICKED ME UP IS THE SAME CLOTHING I WAS WEARING WHEN I WENT INTO THE GREEN CASTLE ON THIRD AVENUE NORTH.

Murder File: Johnnie Avie's 2nd Statement And 1st Confession

My name Johnny Avie, I live at #10 E Olender Homes Galveston, Galveston Texas with my mother and father. I am 18 years old and work on construction.

At about 8:00 am this morning, Saturday the 19th day of September 1970 I went to the old green castle on third avenue north. I went there for the purpose of stealing some money from the people that live there. I know the people but cannot remember their name. I first went around the house and looked through the windows but did not see anyone. I noticed the front door was open, so I went inside and went to the kitchen. I first noticed the lady that lives there was lying in the kitchen floor and was bleeding from the mouth. There was a lot of blood on the floor under her.

I first went to the refrigerator and opened it up and looked inside and then went upstairs to one of the bedrooms and looked for some money. After a while I got scared and started running. I ran out the front door and went to Mr. Johnny McDaniel's house on first Ave north.

The clothing and shoes that I was wearing when the police picked me up is the same clothing I was wearing when I went into the green castle on third avenue north.

This statement gave the police a huge win. Even though Avie was still denying attacking Mrs. Ida, raping her, and murdering her, he did place himself inside of the home during the time when the crime was suspected to have been committed. According to the confession, it would seem like Avie entered The Davison Home shortly after being seen in the area by Officer Gilmore. Also, the time in which Avie admitted to entering the home coincided with the time that the neighbor, Mr. Edward Swann, said that he heard someone scream in the vicinity of The Davison Home.

If his statement was to be believed, however, it would seem that the real killer was still on the loose. Avie was saying yes, he illegally entered the home, but when he did, he found Mrs. Ida Davison already lying on the kitchen floor unconscious and bleeding. It was as if he was saying that some other person committed the crime, and he broke into the home after the crime was committed. The classic "wrong place at the wrong time."

The only problem with his statement was his timeline. Remember, Mr. Don Davison left the home around 7:45 a.m. to go open the family grocery store. If Avie did in fact enter the home around 8:00 a.m., and the statement he gave was true, that made only one of two things possible.

1. The real killer entered the home at 7:45 a.m. after Don left, beat and raped Mrs. Ida in under 15 minutes, then fled the house before Avie was going around the house looking in through the windows, and Avie somehow didn't see him fleeing the scene.

2. Mr. Don C. Davison was the real killer, and he beat and raped his own wife for some unknown reason and then left her bleeding out on the kitchen floor as he headed to work that morning.

Neither one of those scenarios made more sense than the scenario that said Avie was in fact the real killer, so the police knew they needed to continue to press him until he admitted to the murder itself. They no doubt leveraged the fact that he admitted to being inside the home and coupled it with the fact that he had blood on his clothing, to ensure him that they could prove he had sexually assaulted the victim.

For the next 30 minutes the police no doubt impressed upon Avie the immense gravity of the situation and let him know that lying would not help him get away with it. We have all watched police interrogations on either TV or social media. What is one thing that they always do? We can imagine that the TCPD pulled Avie out of his jailcell and took him into a private room. He may or may not have been handcuffed, but with the nature of the crime they were investigating, his lengthy criminal record, and his physical 6'5 stature, I'm certain that the police took their own safety and security into consideration.

In this room, the interrogation would've commenced. They no doubt told Avie that he was in a lot of trouble. More trouble than he had ever been in in his entire life. They would have mentioned some of the evidence they had against him, and they would've quite possibly lied about evidence that didn't even exist. They would have told him how much time he was looking at in prison, and what would happen to him when he got there.

"Listen Johnnie." The cops would have said. "This is serious. We're not going to call your parents to come pick you up like we've done the other times. You're not a juvenile anymore. You're 18. You're a man, Johnnie. And this isn't a disorderly conduct charge. We're talking about cold... blooded... murder."

In my mind's eye I can see the cop leaning back in his chair, and Johnnie Avie hanging his head. I can see him wringing his hands together as his palms began to sweat. His mind racing a million miles per second trying to figure out a story that could get him out of this predicament.

"Someone." The cop would have continued, looking directly at Avie without turning away. "Broke into The Davison

Home, attacked a 75-year-old woman, and beat her until she was unconscious. Then, that same person pulled down her under garments and sexually violated her."

The cop probably leaned back in to close the distance between him and Johnnie.

"And if that wasn't bad enough, the woman died, Johnnie. She's no longer with us. A husband has lost a wife, children have lost a mother, and grandchildren have lost a grandmother. Hell, the entire Texas City community suffered a loss with this murder, Johnnie. Do you even know who Mrs. Ida Davison was? I mean... do you even realize the gravity of the situation you're in?"

Without raising his head, Johnnie probably let those words resonate inside of his spirit. Of course, he knew who the Davison's were. He didn't know anything specific about them, but he knew they were a very powerful family.

"Well," Johnnie responded weakly. "I didn't know her name, but I know about the big green castle, and I know about the family that lives there."

"That family, Johnnie," The cop continued. "Is one of the most powerful families in this city. Hell, they helped to create this city that you yourself grew up in. Now listen Johnnie, we know you did it, and you know you did it. And we know why you're lying about it. You're afraid, ain't ya? Well, listen up Johnnie. We've already processed your clothes. Do you want to know what we found?"

The cop shuffled around the papers on his desk.

"We found blood, Johnnie." He revealed. "And we can prove that the blood found on your shorts and your underwear are a direct match for Mrs. Ida Davison."

The cop paused for a second to let that information sink in and marinate. Johnnie knew that he had blood on his clothes, and now he knew the cops could connect that blood to the victim.

"So, we know you raped her, Johnnie. And unless you tell us your side of the story, you're going to look like a heartless rapist and murderer, and you're going to spend the rest of your natural life in prison."

The police waited for a moment. They wanted the severity of the crime to sink all the way in. They sat there looking at Johnnie Avie as he slowly accepted what he was hearing. As more time passed, he knew that he wasn't going to get out of this situation. He was caught and they were not going to let him go. However, he didn't want to come out and explicitly admit to the murder.

"Ok." Johnnie said reluctantly. "I did have sex with that lady, but I did not kill her. You gotta believe me. I found her like that when I went inside the green castle."

The cops exchanged glances. They knew that he was finally ready to tell them more of the story. They needed it on the record however, so they once again made sure he understood his rights, and then they prepared to take his new statement in which he said he was now willing to admit to the rape. This was the second confession made by Johnnie Avie, in which he gave the police more information about what exactly he did inside of The Davison Home that morning.

My name is ___JOHNNY AVIE___ . I live at ___#10 E. ⬛⬛⬛⬛⬛ OLEANDER HOMES GALVESTON,___

T EXAS WITH MY MOTHER AND FATHER. I AM 18 YEARS OLD AND WORK ON CONSTRUCTION.

AT ABOUT 8:00 AM THIS MORNING, SATURDAY SEPTEMBER 19, 1970 I WENT TO THE OLD GREEN
CASTLE ON THIRD AVENUE NORTH. I WENT THERE FOR THE PURPOSE OF STEALING SOME MONEY FROM THE
PE OPLE THAT LIVE THERE. I KNOW THE PEOPLE BUT CAN NOT REMEMBER THEIR NAME. I FIRST WENT
AROUND THE HOUSE AND LOOKED THROUGH ALL THE WINDOWS BUT DID NOT SEE ANYONE. I NOTICED THE FRONT
DOOR WAS OPEN SO I WENT INSIDE AND WENT TO THE KITCHEN. I SAW THE LADY THAT LIVES THERE
LYING ON THE KITCHEN FLOOR WITH BLOOD ON HER. I SAW THAT SHE WAS HELPLESS SO I RAPED HER.

I ONLY RAPED HER ONCE AND WHEN I FINISHED I WENT TO THE REFRIGERATOR AND OPENED IT UP.
I THEN WENT UP STAIRS TO ONE OF THE BEDROOMS AND LOOKED FOR SOME MONEY.

WHILE I WAS IN THE BEDROOM I GOT SCARED AND STARTED RUNNING. I RAN OUT THE FRONT DOOR
WHICH WAS THE SAME ON I HAD ENTERED. I WENT TO JOHNNY McDANIELS HOUSE ON FIRST AVENUE NORTH
AND WENT TO SLEEP UNTIL AROUND 11:00 AM.

THE CLOTHING I WAS WEARING WHEN THE POLICE PICKED ME UP WAS THE SAME CLOTHING THAT I
WAS WEARING WHEN I WENT INTO THE GREEN CASTLE THIS MORNING.

Murder File: Johnnie Avie's 3rd Statement And 2nd Confession

My name is Johnie Avie. I live at #10 E. Oleander Homes Galveston, Texas with my mother and father. I am 18 years old and work on construction.

At about 8:00 am this morning, Saturday September 19,1970 I went to the old green castle on third avenue north. I went there for the purpose of stealing money from the people that live there. I know the people but can not remember their name. I first went around the house and looked through all the windows but did not see anyone. I noticed the front door was open so I went inside and went to the kitchen. I saw the lady that lives there lying on the kitchen floor with blood on her. I saw that she was helpless so I raped her.

I only raped her once and when I finished I went to the refrigerator and opened it up. I then went upstairs to one of the bedrooms and looked for some money.

While I was in the bedroom I got scared and started running. I ran out the front door which was the same one I had entered. I went to Johnny McDaniel's house on first avenue north and went to sleep until around 11:00 am.

The clothing I was wearing when the police picked me up was the same clothes that I was wearing when I went into the green castle this morning.

When I first read these two confessions, I got the strange feeling like the second confession was only an edited version of the first one. The two confessions are written word for word in the beginning of them, and the narrative only seems to change at the point when Avie says he saw Mrs. Ida lying on the kitchen floor with blood around her. In the second confession, instead of seeing her lying there and then opening up the refrigerator, Avie claims that when he saw her he raped her once and then opened up the refrigerator.

If that was the truth, one is left to wonder why a man would break into a house, find a 75-year-old woman lying in a pool of blood, and then rape her. It is interesting to note that even though Avie had now given two separate confessions, he did not admit to attacking nor killing Mrs. Ida Davison. He maintained that someone else attacked her prior to his entering the premises. One could assume that he was trying to take the charges of burglary and rape while simultaneously avoiding the charge of murder.

This second confession was taken at 9:17 p.m., and even though Avie did not admit to the murder itself, he admitted to enough for the police to charge him with the crime. He had placed himself at the scene of the crime, he admitted to having physical contact with the victim, and he admitted that he did in fact see her as she lay on the floor bleeding out. Also, when he claimed to have entered the house for the purpose of stealing, he had inadvertently given the police a motive. At that point, Avie probably thought he was outsmarting the police, but in fact he had only sealed his fate.

Before the ink was even dry on the confession, the TCPD had once again called Judge Ted Bishop. At 10:10 p.m., the same night of the murder, the judge accepted the formal complaint against Johnnie Avie and charged him with Murder with Malice. At 10:15 p.m., Judge Bishop again advised Avie of his rights and made him aware that he was now being charged with murder, and Avie said that he understood. At that point Johnnie Avie was placed back into his cell, and it would now be on the prosecutor's office to secure a conviction in court.

IN THE NAME AND BY AUTHORITY OF THE STATE OF TEXAS:

BEFORE ME, the undersigned authority, on this day personally appeared _D Devil Oliver, TCPD_

who, after being by me duly sworn, on oath deposes and says: That heretofore, to-wit, on or about the _19x4_

day of _Sept_ A. D., 19 _70_ and before the making and filing of this Complaint, in

the County of _Galveston_ and State of Texas,

JOHNNY AVIE

did then and there unlawfully* _Murder with malice_

against the peace and dignity of the State.

Devil Oliver

Complainant

Sworn to and subscribed before me, this _19th_ day of _Sept_ A. D., 19 _70_

2nd Prt

Justice of the Peace,

Precinct No. _5_ _Galveston_ County, Texas.

*Here describe specifically the offense committed.

Murder File: Johnnie Avie Is Formally Charged With Murder

LAST NAME	FIRST NAME	INITIAL	ALIASES (If several, write them at bottom)		ARREST NO
AVIE	JOHNNY		DOB 8-20-52		51319

RESIDENCE		Pret.	Sex	Color	Age	OCCUPATION
#6- BAY ST.			M F	W N M O	18	CONST.
			X			

Date Time of Arrest	Place Arrested		Pret.	Arresting Officer	Badge No
9-19-70 1717	6th.ST. & 2nd.AVE.S.			MONROE	500

Charge When Booked | Charge Changed to _9-19-70_

OLD TRAFFIC AND ~~MURDER~~ | FORMAL CHARGE OF MURDER W/MALICE FILED WITH JUDGE BISHOP 2210 HRS

FACTS OF ARREST (Describe specific act for which prisoner was arrested)

SUBJ ADVISED OF RIGHTS BY JUDGE BISHOP AT 1830 HRS 9-19-70

SUBJ ADVISED OF RIGHTS BY JUDGE BISHOP AT 2215 HRS 9-19-70

Visited Father 9-20-70 at 9:45 AM

1845 Hr 9-19-70 Subj Ref To use Phone + Requested DORATY No Visitors DTO

1500 HRS 9-21-70 TRANSferred To Co Jail by

Arrest Record | Texas City, Texas Police Dept. | Ident. No.

Oliver + Eden

Murder File: Johnnie Avie Is Formally Charged With Murder

130

For some reason, the next day, September 20, 1970, the police claim that Avie gave yet another statement to the police in which he confessed to striking the victim. This is important because it was the blunt force trauma to the head of the victim that Dr. Weiss determined was the ultimate cause of death. With this new confession, the police acquired a statement from Avie that admitted to all of the pertinent portions of the crime. He admitted to entering the house, he admitted to raping the victim, and now, he had also admitted to inflicting the wound which proved to be fatal.

Subject stated to Judge that he did understand.

Subject confined to jail.

12:05PM 9-20-70

Subject was again advised of his rights after which he admitted entering the house for the purpose of stealing some money. Subject stated he found the victim lying on the floor and proceded to rape her. The victim tried to push him off at which time the subject struck her with his fist in the face. Subject then went upstairs to a bed room and stole some money. Subject stated he then went to the home of Johnie McDaniel Address 109 1st Ave. North and slept until about 11AM and then went to town and got into a dice game with a Bruce Montgomery.

Subject gave a voluntary statement to this effect.

Murder File: Johnnie Avie's 4th Statement And 3rd Confession

Subject was again advised of his rights after which he admitted entering the house for the purpose of stealing some money. Subject stated he found the victim lying on the floor and proceeded to rape her. The victim tried to push him off at which time the subject struck her with his fist in the face.

131

Subject then went upstairs to a bedroom and stole some money. Subject stated he then went to the home Johnnie McDaniel Address 109 1st Ave. North and slept until about 11 AM and then went to town and got into a dice game with a Bruce Montgomery.

Subject gave a voluntary statement to this effect.

40 minutes after giving this new confession, the police asked Avie if he would be willing to submit a sample of his pubic hair and the hairs from his head for testing. Avie agreed and he removed the hair from his own body himself and turned them over to the police who then bagged them and tagged them as evidence. As I stated earlier, this crime took place before DNA testing was popularized, but the police wanted to compare the hair of Avie to the hairs they found at the crime scene and on the body of the victim.

Johnnie Avie sat inside of the Texas City jail for the rest of that day, and then at 3:00 p.m. the next day, September 21, 1970, Avie was cleared through the booking office for transfer to Galveston County Jail. When he left the station, he first was taken to the office of Dr. C.F. Quinn where he was thoroughly examined. The examination did not take long, and at 3:44 p.m. that day, Officer Eden and Officer Oliver transferred Johnnie Avie into the custody of the Galveston County Jail where he was to remain until the conclusion of his case.

Chapter 9

Examining The Evidence Against Johnnie Avie

Even though the police had their prime suspect in custody, and even though they had received a full confession from him, the case was not yet closed. There was still the potential for Johnnie Avie to plead not guilty in court. If he did, the laws of the United States afforded him the opportunity to have a fair and speedy trial and be judged by a jury of his peers. With this in mind, the police proceeded to process all of the evidence they had gathered and run as many tests as they could.

There were three main sources of physical evidence that they examined in this case to try and tie Avie to this crime. One source of evidence came from Avie himself. Another source of evidence came from the body of the victim. The third source of evidence came from the actual crime scene, The Davison Home.

Exhibit "B"1 through B-7, removed from suspect, Johnnie (nmn) AVIE

    B-1 Shirt
    B-2 pants
    B-3 Shorts
    B-4 Sandel, right
    B-5 Sandel, left
    B-6 Pubic hair
    B-7 Hair from head

Murder File: Evidence Taken From Johnnie Avie

The evidence collected from Johnnie Avie, aka Pie, was his shirt, his pants, his shorts, his sandals, his pubic hair, and the hair of his head. His clothes were needed as evidence because it showed that he fit the description of the colored male seen in the area by both the police and two citizens prior to the murder. Also, it was claimed that there was blood on his clothes that was possibly the blood of the victim.

A47360

Exhibit A-1 through A-10, removed from victim, Ida C. DAVISON

A-1 House coat
A-2 Slip
A-3 Underpants
A-4 Hairnet
A-5 Pubic Hair
A-6 Hair from head
A-7 Blood sample
A-8 Vaginal smear
A-9 Finger nail clippings
A-10 Blood scrapings from right hand

Murder File: Evidence Taken From the Body of Mrs. Ida Davison

The evidence collected from the body of Mrs. Ida Davison was her house coat, her slip, her underpants, her hair net, pubic hair, hair from her head, a blood sample, a vaginal smear, fingernail clippings, and blood scrapings from her right hand.

134

Exhibit C-1, from Galveston County Memorial Hospital

C-1 bed sheet

Exhibit D-1 through D-5, evidence found at crime scene, 109 - 3rd Avenue North

D-1 Hair from scene
D-2 Hair from scene
D-3 Teeth from victim (3)
D-4 Grass on kitchen floor
D-5 Sample of grass from yard

Murder File: Evidence Taken From The Davison Home

The evidence collected from the crime scene was two samples of hair (presumable head hair and pubic hair), 3 teeth from the victim which where scattered on the floor, grass on the kitchen floor, and a sample of grass from the yard. One piece of evidence that is not listed here is a palm print Lt. Saragoza found on the stove. The police wanted to analyze the print in the hopes that it could help them identify the killer.

All of this evidence, with the exception of the palm print found on the stove, was sent to a chemist and toxicologist in Houston for testing. Police Chief Rankin DeWalt personally submitted it on September 21, 1970. It took a couple of weeks for all of the tests to be completed, but on October 6, 1970, Police Chief DeWalt received his reply from the lab. I wasn't there when he read the letter that the lab sent to him, but I can imagine he was not too pleased with what it said. Virtually none of the evidence they collected would help them in an actual trial.

The lab couldn't prove that that blood found on the suspect came from the victim, they couldn't prove that the hair found on the victim came from the suspect, and they couldn't even prove that the suspect had left traces of his semen inside of the victim from the rape. Regardless of whether Avie committed the crime or not, it's not what you know, it's what you can prove. Yes, they had the confession in their arsenal, but a jury would want to see physical evidence connecting Avie to the crime.

Here's the letter that Police Chief Rankin DeWalt received that told him that basically all of his evidence was useless.

Murder File: The Lab Gives Chief DeWalt The Results Of Their Tests Pg 1

Due to contamination by blood the vaginal smear was not suitable
for seminal stain determination.

We will retain the evidence in our files until we hear from you
of a final disposition.

Anytime we may be of service, please feel free to call.

Yours very truly,

Major Jerry E. Miller
Commander, Region 2

By: *Dennis R. Ramsey*

Dennis R. Ramsey
Chemist & Toxicologist
Houston, Region 2

DRR:sr

cc: Galveston Co., DA

Murder File: The Lab Gives Chief DeWalt The Results Of Their Tests Pg 2

Chief Rankin L. DeWalt

928 – 5th Avenue North

Texas City, Texas 77590

Dear Sir:

On September 21, 1970 you personally submitted the following evidence: A house coat, slip, underpants, hairnet, pubic hair, head hair, a wet blood sample, a vaginal smear, fingernail clippings, and blood scrapings all from the victim. You also submitted from the subject a shirt, pair of pants, pair of boxer shorts, a pair of sandals, pubic hair, and head hair.

137

From the crime scene you submitted hair samples, teeth from the victim, grass found on the kitchen floor, and a sample of grass from the yard.

You requested that we make comparisons and analyses to determine the suspects involvement in this crime.

We have made our examination and wish to report that the blood sample taken from the victim at the hospital was of type O origin, that the human blood stains were found on the shirt, pair of pants, and shorts of the suspect, and that no blood stains were found on the suspect's sandals. None of the stains were suitable for typing procedures. We would like to report also that human blood stains were found on the house coat, slip, under pants, and fingernail clippings of the victim. The crusts from the right hand of the victim were also human blood stains. None of the stains from the victim were suitable for typing procedures. The blood on the sheet from the hospital was also unsuitable for typing procedures. We would also like to report that none of the hair found at the scene showed any similarity to either the head hair or the pubic hair samples taken from the suspect. The grass found on the kitchen floor was molded and not suitable for a valid comparison to the grass taken from the yard.

Due to contamination by blood the vaginal smear was not suitable for seminal stain determination.

We will retain the evidence in our files until we hear from you of a final disposition.

Anytime we may be of service, please feel free to call.

Yours very truly,

Major Jerry E. Miller

Commander, Region 2

By: Dennis R. Ramsey

Dennis R. Ramsey

Chemist & Toxicologist

Houston, Region 2

DRR: sr

Cc: Galveston Co., DA

This letter was a devastating blow to the Texas City Police. In essence, the report stated that the lab could not determine if the blood found underneath the fingernails of the victim was indeed the blood of the suspect. Also, they could not determine if the blood found on the suspect was indeed the blood of the victim. One thing that the report did confirm, however, was that Avie had human blood on his clothing. He had human blood on his shirt, his shorts, and his underwear.

There were no wounds found on the body of Johnnie Avie, so the question became, where did the blood found on his clothes come from? If not from the victim, then where? According to the confession, Avie admitted to finding the victim on the floor and raping her, so one could draw the conclusion that the blood on his clothes belonged to Mrs. Ida. Even if he tried to come up with a convincing lie about the origin of the blood on his shirt, he would be hard pressed to explain away the blood found on the front of his boxers.

139

Another interesting fact which we can glean from the evidence is that Mrs. Ida had tried her best to fight her attacker off. This was evident by the dried blood discovered beneath her fingernails. She did not go down without a fight, even though she was 75 years old and understandably frail. This made a particular part of Avie's confession ring true.

He said, "The victim tried to push him off at which time the subject struck her with his fist in the face."

Perhaps when Mrs. Ida tried to push him off of her, some of his blood got lodged beneath her fingernails. Some of this was speculation, however. Yes, the police had the confession, but they had no scientific data to link Avie to the crime. To make matters worse, some of the evidence seemed to exclude Avie from the suspect pool.

The report concluded that, "*none of the hair found at the scene showed any similarity to either the head hair or the pubic hair samples taken from the suspect.*"

That was another devastating blow to Chief DeWalt. Remember, the police took hair samples from the body of Mrs. Ida Davison, and they also took hair samples from Johnnie Avie. The official report stated that the hair taken from Avie did not show any similarity to the hair found on the body of the victim. Yet another crucial piece of evidence failed to connect Avie to the crime. In fact, the conclusion of the examination of the hair samples would lead one to believe that perhaps Avie did not commit the crime. After all, if the hairs on the body of the victim did not belong to Avie, and they did not belong to Mrs. Ida, then who exactly did they belong to?

The general public was never made aware of this fact, but the question must be asked, did the hair belong to a different suspect. Was there some unnamed killer who committed this heinous act, and Avie was merely coerced into a confession by a police force hell bent on arresting a suspect? Considering the fact that the only other real suspect was the husband of Mrs. Ida, I wonder if the police ever compared the hair and blood samples to Mr. Don Davison.

In my opinion, even if someone suggested that the hairs be compared to the hairs of Mr. Don Davison, Police Chief Rankin DeWalt wouldn't dare subject that man to such scrutiny. As stated earlier, not only was Chief DeWalt a masonic brother of Mr. Don Davison, but even the mayor of Texas City was a masonic brother of Mr. Davison. And Mr. Davison outranked both of them within the lodge. So, it would take an act of God Himself to get the police to actually investigate a former Master Mason of the same lodge the Police Chief and Mayor were members of.

Also, it just didn't seem logical that Mr. Davison would assault his wife of 50 years, rape her, and then leave her for dead. The only other possible explanation for the evidence was that Mr. Davison assaulted his wife in the midst of some argument, and Johnnie Avie found her lying on the floor bleeding out when he broke into the house just as he claimed. Then, finding Mrs. Ida incapacitated, Avie used the opportunity to live out his sick and twisted fantasy of sexually assaulting a helpless woman.

I must admit that in my personal opinion it does not make sense that Mr. Davison assaulted his wife and Avie broke into the house shortly after. It makes more sense that Avie broke into the house, found Mrs. Ida in the kitchen, attacked her, raped her, and then left her for dead as he searched the house for money and valuables. I'm neither the police, the judge, the jury, nor the prosecutor, however. And it is not my intention in this work to play the role of either. I am simply presenting the facts, presenting the theories, and stating what is clearly stated in the official records.

Regardless of what actually happened on September 19, 1970, the Texas City police did not have as much evidence as they originally believed they had. Virtually all of it was inconclusive. The only seemingly conclusive evidence that the lab examined seemed to imply that someone other than Avie was the actual culprit. This evidence was the hair collected from the body of the victim, and the hairs collected from Avie himself.

In spite of all of this inconclusive evidence, later on in the month of October, the Grand Jury still ruled that there was enough evidence to formally indict Johnnie Avie, aka Pie, for the crime of Murder with Malice. It appears that they made this decision based primarily on the confession of Avie himself, and the witnesses who saw him acting strangely in the area at the time of the murder.

Teen Indicted
In Slaying Case

A Galveston County Grand Jury has returned a murder with malice indictment against Johnnie Avie, 18, of Galveston, accusing him of the Sept. 19 murder of Mrs. Don C. (Ida) Davison, 75.

The indictment was returned in Judge Donald Markle's 10th District Court.

Mrs. Davison, member of a pioneer Texas City family, was found beaten and bleeding from head wounds on the floor of her kitchen at her home at 109 3rd Ave. North, Texas City.

She was taken to Galveston County Memorial Hospital where she died the same day. An autopsy showed Mrs. Davison died from a skull fracture, and Dr. Kurt G. Weiss, medical examiner, said the elderly woman had been criminally assaulted.

Galveston Daily News October 21, 1970

Teen Indicted In Slaying Case

A Galveston County Grand Jury has returned a murder with malice indictment against Johnnie Avie, 18, of Galveston, accusing him of the Sept. 19 murder of Mrs. Don C. (Ida) Davison, 75.

The indictment was returned in Judge Donald Markle's 10th District Court.

Mrs. Davison, member of a pioneer Texas City family, was found beaten and bleeding from head wounds on the floor of her kitchen at her home at 109 3rd Ave. North, Texas City.

She was taken to Galveston County Memorial hospital where she died the same day. An autopsy showed Mrs. Davison died from a skull fracture, and Dr. Kurt G. Weiss, medical examiner, said the elderly woman had been assaulted.

In October of 1970, just a month after his arrest, Avie was formally indicted by the Grand Jury for the crime of Murder with Malice. For those of you who do not know, whenever someone is arrested by the police and charged with a crime, there are no immediate guarantees that they will one day stand trial for that charge. Everyone who is arrested must first be formally indicted by the Grandu Jury. But what exactly is a "Grand Jury?"

According to the Cornell Law School, A grand jury is a group of people selected to sit on a jury that decide whether the prosecutor's evidence provides probable cause to issue an indictment. An indictment formally charges a person with committing a crime and begins the criminal prosecution process.

In the United States, a grand jury consists of 16 to 23 people. Grand juries convene for a period of one month up to one year. The grand jury proceedings are held in private; the suspected criminal actor is usually not present at the proceedings.

The grand jury acts as an investigative body, acting independently of either prosecuting attorney or judge.

Criminal prosecutors present the case to the grand jury. The prosecutors attempt to establish probable cause to believe that a criminal offense has been committed. The grand jury may request that the court compel further evidence, including witness testimony and subpoenas of documents. The grand jury is generally free to pursue its investigations unhindered by external influence or supervision.

Basically, the Grand Jury decides if there is enough evidence to actually try an individual for the crime they are being accused of. They look at the evidence collected by the police and determine if this evidence should be considered by a judge and jury in the court of law. Some people who are arrested are never indicted for the crime, and they are released and never have to appear in court. Others, like Avie, are officially indicted, and they have to fight for their freedom. This is why the police gather as much evidence as possible when a crime is committed. The evidence, or lack thereof, can make or break an indictment hearing.

Chapter 10

The D.A. Seeks The Death Penalty For Johnnie Avie

Once Avie received the news that he was formally indicted for the crime of killing Mrs. Ida, the next step was to wait on the prosecutor's office to offer him a plea deal. The prosecutor will almost always give the defendant the option to plead guilty to the crime they are accused of committing for a lesser sentence. They do this to keep the court system from becoming backed up with too many people awaiting a trial date. As Avie sat inside of his cell in the Galveston County Jail eating prison food and wearing prison clothes, he no doubt sat in anxious anticipation of the deal that the prosecutor would offer him for his murder charge.

Unfortunately for Avie, the prosecutor assigned to his case was a no-nonsense type of prosecutor who had no sympathy for a man who would beat and murder a 75-year-old woman. Not to mention the victim in this case was one of the most well known and loved in all of Texas City. If he didn't punish Avie to the fullest extent of the law, he risked making enemies of one of the most powerful families in Texas City. He also risked making enemies of all the people who were demanding justice for Mrs. Ida Davison. As stated earlier, Mrs. Ida was the wife of a man who not only was the descendant of a man who helped found Texas City, but her husband was also a former Master Mason of the lodge that the police chief and the current Mayor of Texas City were members of.

If this man, Mr. Don C. Davison, could not get justice for his murdered wife, then who could?

It appeared that everything was working against Avie. And if his confession was to be believed, he had messed with the wrong family. There was no chance of him coming out of this unscathed. A few days after his indictment, Johnnie Avie found out just how serious his situation was. The prosecutor in his case was a man named Jules Damiani, and Damiani had zero sympathy for Avie. His only concern was bringing justice to the Davison family. The family who had lost a mother, grandmother, wife, Methodist Christian, Garden Club Member, and community advocate.

An article which ran in the Galveston Daily News October 24, 1970, put the entire county on notice that Damiani wanted Avie to die for what he had done. No amount of time in prison was a sufficient punishment. He believed that Avie should lose his life just as Mrs. Ida lost her life. But who could blame him? If Avie did in fact commit this most heinous crime, he deserved an extremely severe punishment. And at that time in Texas, the most severe punishment was to be strapped down to a wooden chair and electrocuted until you were dead. So, Damiani sought to have Avie electrocuted.

Damiani To Seek 'Chair' In Trial

Criminal District Attorney Jules Damiani announced in open court Friday he will seek the electric chair for Johnnie Avie, 18, of Galveston and Texas City, in the slaying of Mrs. Don C. (Ida) Davison, 75.

In a habeas corpus hearing before 10th District Judge Donald Markle Friday, Damiani introduced a formal notice into the record that he will seek the death penalty for Avie.

Mrs. Davison was fatally beaten at her home at 109 3rd Ave. North in Texas City on Sept. 19.

Judge Markle denied the writ of habeas corpus, and ordered Avie held without bond. Avie was indicted by a Galveston County grand jury earlier this month.

Defense lawyer Ted Allmond, who sought the habeas corpus hearing, apparently, to probe the state's case against his client, battled against admission of a statement made by Avie into the record of the hearing.

Dr. Kurt G. Weiss, an assistant county medical examiner, testified that Mrs. Davison died from a fractured skull that was "compatable with a beating by fists." He also testified extensive contusions and abrasions, and that it appeared

See DAMIANI, Page 10

Weather

GALVESTON AREA — Partly cloudy and mild today through Sunday. High today and Sunday, mid - 70s Island, near 80 Mainland. Low tonight, upper 60s Island, mid-60s Mainland.

BOATING — Small craft warnings are in effect for rough seas and gusty offshore winds. Variable, mostly northerly, winds, 10-18 mph, diminishing today and becoming southerly, 8-18 mph Sunday. Waters will be choppy today and slightly choppy tonight and Sunday. Offshore wave heights, 7-10 feet, subsiding slowly today and becoming 3-5 feet tonight and Sunday.

WATER TEMPERATURE — 72 degrees.

FISHING — Not so good.

LATEST Available TC-LM sampler reading: 64 micrograms per cubic meter.

Galveston Daily News October 24, 1970

Damiani To Seek 'Chair'

[Continued from Page 1]

she had been raped.

. He said, in cross examination by Allmond, that there was no evidence of heart disease.

Texas City police officer Darrell Oliver, who said he had known Mrs. Davison for 20 years, testified he took three statements from the defendant. He testified the defendant was wearing bloody clothing when he was arrested.

There was some discussion about whether the defendant had been properly warned of his rights in Allmond's fight to exclude the statement which was introduced. Two other statements were not introduced, but Allmond examined them.

The left-handed defendant, who was a construction worker, in the statement introduced in the habeas corpus hearing, is accused of saying he took some "Christmas tree" pills and smoked "two sticks of marijuana" before going to the Davison House which he called the "old green mansion" to steal money.

In the statement, the defendant allegedly said he hit Mrs. Davison and raped her on the kitchen floor, then left, after taking coins from the house.

Allmond asked Oliver if he knew whether any fingerprints were taken from the Davison house. Oliver said "yes."

Allmond: "And were they identified as Avie's?"

Oliver: "It is my understanding they were."

Galveston Daily News October 24, 1970

Damiani To Seek 'Chair' In Trial

Criminal District Attorney Jules Damiani announced in open court Friday he will seek the electric chair for Johnnie Avie, 18, of Galveston and Texas City, in the slaying of Mrs. Don C. (Ida) Davison, 75.

In a habeas corpus hearing before 10th District Judge Donald Markle, Friday, Damiani introduced a formal notice into the record that he will seek the death penalty for Avie.

Mrs. Davison was fatally beaten at her home at 109 3rd Ave. North in Texas City on Sept. 19.

Judge Markle denied the writ of Habeas Corpus and ordered Avie held without bond. Avie was indicted by a Galveston County grand jury earlier this month.

Defense lawyer Ted Allmond, who sought the habeas corpus hearing, apparently, to probe the state's case against his client, battled against admission of a statement made by Avie into the record of the hearing.

Dr. Kurt G. Weiss, an assistant county medical examiner, testified that Mrs. Davison died from a fractured skull that was "compatible with a beating by fists." He also testified extensive contusions and abrasions, and that it appeared she had been raped.

He said, in cross examination by Allmond, that there was no evidence of heart disease.

Texas City police officer Darrell Oliver, who said he had known Mrs. Davison for 20 years, testified he took three statements from the defendant. He testified the defendant was wearing bloody clothing when he was arrested.

There was some discussion about whether the defendant had been properly warned of his rights in Allmond's fight to exclude the statement which was introduced. Two other statements were not introduced, but Allmond examined them.

The left-handed defendant, who was a construction worker, in the statement introduced in the habeas corpus, is accused of saying he took some "Christmas tree" pills and smoked "two sticks of marijuana" before going to the Davison House which he called the "old green mansion" to steal money.

In the statement, the defendant allegedly said he hit Mrs. Davison and raped her on the kitchen floor, then left, after taking coins from the house.

Allmond asked Oliver if he knew whether any fingerprints were taken from the Davison house. Oliver said "yes."

Allmond: "And were they identified as Avie's?"

Oliver: "It is my understanding they were."

Although Avie had given several confessions to the police admitting that he did in fact enter The Davison Home on the morning of the murder, strike Mrs. Davison with his fist, rape her on the kitchen floor, and then steal around $4 worth of coins out of the home, when he was asked in court how did he wish to plea, Avie pled 'not guilty'. Perhaps, regardless of those facts, he was actually an innocent man sitting in prison for the crimes of another. Perhaps, even though he knew he committed the crime, he thought he could outmaneuver the justice system and beat the case at trial. Or perhaps, he knew he committed the crime, he knew he would be found guilty of the crime, and he simply wanted to make his inevitable conviction more difficult to ascertain.

Whatever his reasons were, Avie said that he was innocent, and he maintained that stance for two years following his arrest. His defense lawyer, Ted Allmond, definitely had an uphill battle representing Avie, but he did have a few tricks up his sleeve. It was his job to try and punch holes in the case of the prosecution. Remember, a person is technically innocent until proven guilty in the court of law. So, until there was an official conviction, Avie was innocent, even though he admitted guilt in his multiple confessions.

When his defense lawyer reviewed the evidence against Avie, he quickly realized that the strongest evidence the state had against his client was the confessions themselves. All of the other evidence came back as inclusive. Yes, Avie had blood on his clothing when he was arrested, but in 1970, the best test they could run to compare those blood samples to the blood of the victim was to test and see if the blood types matched. They knew that Mrs. Ida Davison had type O blood, so they tested to see if the blood stains on Avie's clothes were type O as well. As stated earlier, the lab which conducted the tests could not determine the blood type of the blood found on Avie's clothing.

That meant that the blood on his clothing was only circumstantial evidence. It could have come from a multitude of different sources. It could've been the blood of Avie himself. Likewise, the blood found beneath the fingernails of the victim could not be tested to confirm it was the same blood type as Avie. If DNA testing was available back then, the evidence would have told us much more, but unfortunately that is not the case. Also, the lab stated that the hairs found on the victim were in no way similar to the hair samples taken from Avie.

Thus, the state's case hinged on the confessions. Without them, it would be near impossible to prove guilt beyond a shadow of a doubt. And even the confessions themselves had problems. For starters, the police took around 3 or 4 statements from Avie. His first statement was that he did not commit the crime, and he knew nothing about it. His subsequent confessions were all very similar to each other, but they differed in key respects. It seemed like every time a new statement was taken, more details were added to the previous one taken. These facts caused Avie's lawyer to doubt the credibility and legitimacy of the confessions.

Was Avie somehow being coerced by the police to incriminate himself?

Was he being threatened or physically assaulted?

Were all of those statements really what he said?

Were the Texas City Police trying to charge Avie with the crime to protect the real killer? A killer who held significant sway within the city.

When someone reads over those statements, it almost feels like after each one, the police knew that they needed more information in order to charge him with murder. Yes, burglary was a crime, and it was good for the case that in the first confession Avie admitted to entering the home, but they didn't want to charge him for burglary. They wanted to charge him with murder. So, they went and questioned him again.

This time, they were successful in getting Avie to confess that he raped Mrs. Ida, but again, a rape charge is not what they wanted. It was critical to the case, however. They got him to admit to entering the home illegally and sexually assaulting the victim, but the autopsy reported that the cause of death was blunt force trauma. So, in essence, they needed Avie to confess that he was the cause of the blunt force trauma. Remember, Avie was maintaining that when he entered the home, the victim was already lying on the floor bleeding from her head and mouth.

The police eventually went back to Avie again, and they got him to confess that while in the process of raping Mrs. Ida, she tried to fight him off, and so he punched her in the face with his fist. That is what sealed his fate. Defense lawyer Ted Allmond knew this. He knew that without those confessions, his client could possibly go free. That's why in the Habeas Corpus hearing held on October 23, 1970, Ted Allmond attacked the very validity of those confessions and tried to get them thrown out.

He claimed that Avie wasn't properly read his rights, and thus the confessions were not admissible in court. The prosecutor, Jules Damiani, argued that Avie was advised of his rights several times and he even signed documents stating that he was read his rights and that he understood what his rights were. All of this, the prosecution claimed, was done in the presence of Texas City police officers and Judge Ted Bishop.

Both sides fought hard. Everyone involved knew that these proceedings would either make or break the case. If the confessions were allowed in court, it would be almost impossible for Avie to go free. If the confessions were thrown out based on a technicality, Johnnie Avie would have a really good chance of beating the case. In all honesty, the Habeas Corpus court proceedings would determine if Mrs. Ida Davison would get the justice that she rightfully deserved. No human being deserves to die like she did. Especially a 75-year-old grandmother.

On October 23, 1970, the legal war took place. Defense lawyer Ted Allmond faced off with Criminal District Attorney Jules Damiani. The battlefield for this confrontation was the 10th Judicial District Court. Presiding over the proceedings was the Honorable Judge Markle. It was his job to ensure that things did not turn into an all-out melee. There were only two people subpoenaed as witnesses to this showdown. The man who performed the autopsy of Mrs. Ida Davison, Dr. Kurt Weiss, and one of the first officers to arrive at the crime scene, Officer Deril Oliver. Johnnie Avie was also in attendance, but he did not speak during the proceedings.

What I would like to do at this point is take you into the courtroom itself so you can hear for yourself exactly what was said. It's one thing for myself or a newspaper article to give you a summary of what transpired, but it is another thing entirely for you to read the actual court transcripts with your own eyes. That way you can draw your own conclusions from the evidence presented, and you can determine if the confessions of Johnnie Avie should have been allowed in as evidence in his future trial.

Murder File: Actual Court Transcripts From Habeas Corpus Hearing

INDEX TO
TRANSCRIPT OF TESTIMONY

- - -

---000000---

---oooOooo---

157

NO. 31,252

THE STATE OF TEXAS	§	IN THE DISTRICT COURT OF
VS.	§	GALVESTON COUNTY, TEXAS
JOHNNIE AVIE	§	TENTH JUDICIAL DISTRICT

- - -

HEARING ON APPLICATION
FOR WRIT OF HABEAS CORPUS

- - -

APPEARANCES:

HONORABLE JULES DAMIANI
        Criminal District Attorney for
        Galveston County, Texas

FOR THE STATE OF TEXAS

HONORABLE TED ROBINSON ALLMOND
        National Hotel Building
        Galveston, Texas

FOR THE DEFENDANT

- - -

1   BE IT REMEMBERED That on the 23rd day of
2 October, A. D. 1970, in the Tenth Judicial District Court,
3 Galveston County, Texas, the following proceedings were
4 had before the Honorable Donald M. Markle, Judge of said
5 Court, as follows:
6
7 COURT:
8   This is Cause No. 31,252, the State of Texas against
9   Johnnie Avie. This is a hearing on application for
10   Writ of Habeas Corpus filed by Johnnie Avie on October
11   19, 1970, and set for hearing this morning.
12   Let the record show that the State is represented
13   by Mr. Jules Damiani, Criminal District Attorney of
14   Galveston County, Texas. That the Defendant is present
15   and with him is his attorney, Mr. Ted R. Allmond.
16   Is that Johnnie Avie?
17 MR. ALLMOND:
18   That's correct, Your Honor.
19 COURT:
20   He is represented by his attorney, Mr. Ted Allmond.
21   Is the applicant ready for the hearing?
22 MR. ALLMOND:
23   That's correct, Your Honor.
24 COURT:
25   Is the State ready?

1 MR. DAMIANI:

2   Yes, Your Honor.

3 COURT:

4   All right. Are there any witnesses to be sworn?

5 MR. DAMIANI:

6   Yes, Your Honor- Mr. Oliver- and Dr. Weiss. Take the

7   stand, please.

8 COURT:

9   You can step up here, please, and swear in the

10   witnesses, please. Hold up your right hand- raise

11   your right hand- (The two witnesses who had stepped

12   forward, and raised their hands, are sworn as

13   witnesses in this case by the Deputy District Clerk).

14   Does anyone wish the Rule to be invoked?

15 MR. ALLMOND:

16   The Defendant- the Relator does, Your Honor.

17 COURT:

18   All right. The Rule has been invoked, and that means

19   the witnesses will have to remain outside the Court-

20   room except when they are in here testifying, and

21   they are not to discuss this case with anyone, until

22   this hearing is over with, unless you get permission

23   from me to do so. You are not to receive any report

24   of what goes on in here during the hearing when you

25   are not in the Courtroom.

1   All right. Who will be the first witness?
2   MR. DAMIANI:
3   Dr. Weiss, Your Honor.
4   COURT:
5   All right- if you will a seat there in the witness
6   stand, and the other witnesses will remain outside
7   of the Courtroom until called in.
8
9
10   DR. KURT WEISS, called by the State, after
11 first being duly sworn, testified as follows:
12
13   - - -
14 MR. DAMIANI:
15   Your Honor, in accordance with Article 114 of the
16   Code of Criminal Procedure of the State of Texas,
17   the State of Texas at this time files this notice
18   with the Court- (Mr. Damiani hands paper to the Court
19   and a copy to Mr. Allmond).
20 COURT:
21   All right. The State has filed notice that it will
22   seek the death penalty in this case. I will ask the
23   District Clerk to place the file mark thereon- (This
24   is done).
25 MR. DAMIANI:

1   Mr. Reporter- (Copy of Indictment is marked S-1,

2   initialed Ray O'N, and dated 10-23-70).

3   Your Honor, at this time, the State would

4   introduce into evidence State's Exhibit 1 for identi-

5   fication, as State's Exhibit 1- the same being a

6   certified copy of the indictment returned in this file

7   numbered cause.

8 MR. ALLMOND:

9   There is no objection, Your Honor.

10 COURT:

11   It's admitted- (Instrument marked S-1, initialed Ray

12   O'N, dated 10-23-70, appears herein attached to the

13   following page).

At this point there was one page missing in the transcript files that I was unable to acquire. Fortunately, we still have the complete line of questioning that Dr. Weiss was subjected to.

1 Reporter's Note:

2   The witness, Curt Weiss, had been sworn and had taken

3 his place on the witness stand, and Mr. Damiani proceeds

4 to examine the witness as follows:

5 ON DIRECT EXAMINATION BY MR. DAMIANI:

6

7 MR. DAMIANI:

8   Will you state your name, please sir?

9 A. My name is Kurt Weiss.

10 Q. What is your occupation, sir?

11 A. My occupation is- physician.

12 Q. And where do you practice, Doctor?

13 A. I practice here in Galveston.

14 Q. And where did you obtain your medical education- your

15   schooling, sir?

16 A. I went to medical school in Hamburg, Germany, most of

17   the time.

18 Q. And do you have any specialty- special form of medicine

19   which you practice?

20 A. My specialty is pathology.

21 Q. Do you hold any official capacity with the County of

22   Galveston?

23 A. I am Assistant Medical Examiner of Galveston County.

24 Q. How long have you been Assistant Medical Examiner of

25   Galveston County, sir?

1 A. Since about June 22, of this year.

2 Q. Who is the Medical Examiner for Galveston County?

3 A. Dr. Robert Bucklin.

4 Q. Doctor, are you duly licensed to practice medicine,

5 in the State of Texas?

6 A. Yes, sir.

7 Q. Now, in your practice as pathologist, have you had

8 occasion to perform post mortems on deceased persons?

9 A. Yes, sir.

10 Q. Has that been on frequent or infrequent occasions?

11 A. It was on frequent occasions, I would think.

12 A. I will ask you, sir, whether or not, on or about the

13 19th day of September, 1970, you had occasion to

14 perform an autopsy on the person of Ida C. Davidson?

15 A. Yes, sir.

16 Q. Where was that autopsy performed, Dr. Weiss?

17 A. It was performed in John Sealy Hospital.

18 Q. And about what age would you estimate Mrs. Davidson

19 to be, sir?

20 A. She was around seventy.

21 Q. Around seventy, you say?

22 A. I would say seventy- uh-huh- seventy-five- I could

23 not say for sure.

24 Q. What is your best estimate of her age?

25 A. She was seventy-five.

1   Q. Now--

2   A. She was about seventy-five.

3   Q. Now, about what time of day or night did you perform

4   this post mortem, sir.

5   A. It was in the afternoon, I think- at 3:25- we started.

6   Q. Where was that performed?

7   A. In the morgue of John Sealy Hospital.

8   Q. How large a woman was Mrs. Davison?

9   A. I would say she was a heavy woman. I'd estimate her

10   to weigh 170 lbs.

11   Q. As a result of your autopsy on the person of Ida C.

12   Davison, did you form an opinion as to the cause of

13   death?

14   A. Yes, sir.

15   Q. What was that, sir?

16   A. I feel like she died from a fracture of the skull.

17   Q. Did you note any abrasions or contusions on or about

18   her person?

19   A. Yes, I noted rather specific contusions and abrasions

20   on the right side of her neck and on the right side of

21   her face.

22   Q. So, I will ask you whether or not that skull fracture

23   that you testified to, and the contusions and abrasions

24   could have been the result of being hit with a fist?

25   A. I feel it could be caused by being hit with a fist.

1	Q.	Did you notice any other abrasions on or about her
2		person?
3	A.	There were some lacerations of the vagina.
4	Q.	You say lacerations of the vagina?
5	A.	Yes, sir.
6	Q.	Was that compatible with the entrance of a foreign
7		object?
8	A.	Yes.
9	Q.	Was there extensive damage to the vagina?
10	A.	Yes, I think there was extensive damage to the vagina
11		in this case.
12	Q.	And it is your testimony, sir, that the primary cause
13		of death- was a fracture of the skull?
14	A.	Yes, sir.
15	Q.	The events about which you've testified, occurred here
16		in the county of Galveston- the post mortem?
17	A.	Yes, sir.
18	Q.	Thank you, Doctor. We pass the witness.
19		
20		
21		
22		
23		
24		
25		

-11-
A47360

ON CROSS EXAMINATION BY MR. ALIMOND:

Q. Did you determine whether or not there were other contributing factors that might have brought about this death?

A. There were other contributing factors. Other contributing factors were the hemorrhage into the soft tissues of the neck, on the right, and the hemorrhage or bleeding into the vagina.

Q. Doctor, did you make any observation in regard to the heart of this woman?

A. Yes, sir.

Q. Did you find anything abnormal or unusual about the condition of her heart, at the time of her autopsy?

A. Let me look through my notes- (Witness looks through his notes). I did not notice any areas of infarctions or lesions, or areas of scars, or recent areas of necrosis or infarction, or what we call an infarct- an infarct of the heart- I did not find those. There was some arterial sclerosis- hardening of the arteries.

Q. Then, Doctor, it is your opinion that this woman did not have any sort of heart condition that might have contributed to her demise- is that my understanding?

A. Under the circumstances- no.

Q. Now, I did not quite understand Mr. Damiani when he

1   asked you- did you say that the contusions of the side

2   of the face and neck were brought about by some sort of

3   a blow- is that correct?

4 A. They were compatible with being inflicted by a fist,

5   or by any other object, or by an arm- but the object

6   was not sharp and did not leave any inference and did

7   not leave any impression marks.

8 Q. It would have been compatible with a human fist- a

9   human fist could have done this- is that correct?

10 A. Yes- the human fist or human arm.

11 Q. Did you, Doctor, make any examination of the woman's

12   teeth?

13 A. We looked at the teeth, from the outside, and some of

14   the upper teeth were natural and present, and on the

15   lower jaw, she had partial artificial dentures.

16 Q. Were there any other teeth missing when you examined

17   her?

18 A. Well, the natural teeth were missing where the

19   artificial plates were. Is that what you mean, sir?

20 Q. Sir, if there were any teeth missing, were they

21   artificial dentures- this is what I mean.

22 A. One of the artificial teeth from the plate was broken,

23   and there was an opening.

24 Q. Did you notice whether or not any of her natural

25   teeth were missing- the ones that were still her teeth?

168

1   A.   Well, they were missing- otherwise, they would not have

2   been replaced by artificial dentures. Is that what

3   you mean, or--

4   Q.   Sir, what I am inquiring of you- I understand that

5   part of one of her dentures was missing.

6   A.   Yes.

7   Q.   Were there any other teeth missing?

8   A.   I did not notice.

9   Q.   Doctor, considering her age and size, do you think

10   that the blow or blows that you say caused this skull

11   fracture, could they have been caused by one such blow?

12   A.   Possibly- but possibly- and I think more likely, more

13   than one blow- maybe two.

14   Q.   But it is possible that one blow could have brought

15   about this skull fracture that you say was the

16   primary cause of her death?

17   A.   Yes, sir. It is not necessarily caused by the blow.

18   It may be caused by the fact that it threw over the

19   woman- by the fact that the woman fell over, and then

20   hit the floor.

21   Q.   All right. So, it is possible that the damage which

22   was done to her, could have been done by something

23   other than the human fist- such as by falling and

24   striking an object- is that correct?

25   A.   Yes, sir- the skull fracture, that is.

1	Q. It would be possible, if I were to be walking across
2	this room, and slip and fall, and I could hit a chair
3	and bring about the same kind of damage that you
4	describe- is that correct?
5	A. You can bring about by the fall, the skull fracture.
6	You would not bring about the hemorrhages in the neck,
7	which I described.
8	Q. Doctor, do you have any idea- do you have a medical
9	opinion as to how long this woman would have lived,
10	after receiving the damage to her neck and jaw?
11	A. Yes.
12	Q. How long?
13	A. A woman like this can live several hours with skull
14	fracture.
15	Q. Do you know the exact time of death, Doctor?
16	A. I know she was taken to County Memorial Hospital,
17	but I do not recall the exact time of death. My
18	notice was 12 o'clock noon, the same day- September
19	19th.
20	Q. And you saw her on the afternoon of the 19th, around
21	3 o'clock?
22	A. Yes, sir.
23	Q. So, it would have been some three or three and a half
24	hours after she was taken in, that you examined her?
25	A. Yes, sir.

170

1   Q. Pass the witness.

2   MR. DAMIANI:

3   I have no further questions, Your Honor.

4   COURT:

5   Do you want this witness to remain, or do you want

6   him to be excused?

7   MR. DAMIANI:

8   He may be excused on the part of the State.

9   MR. ALLMOND:

10   He may be excused, Your Honor.

11   COURT:

12   Thank you, Doctor.

13

14   - - -

15

16

17   DERIL OLIVER, called by the State, after first

18 being duly sworn, testified as follows:

19

20

21 ON DIRECT EXAMINATION BY MR. DAMIANI:

22

23   Q. Would you state your name, please sir?

24   A. Deril Oliver.

25   Q. Mr. Oliver, what is your occupation, sir?

1   A. I'm a police officer.

2   Q. And by whom are you employed, please, sir?

3   A. City of Texas City.

4   Q. How long have you been a police officer with the

5   city of Texas City?

6   A. Approximately eight years.

7   Q. I take it then, sir, that you were a police officer

8   on or about the 19th day of September, 1970?

9   A. Yes, sir, I was.

10 Q. Officer, did you have occasion on that day to go to a

11   residence at 109 Third Avenue North in Texas City?

12 A. Yes, sir, I did.

13 Q. Approximately what time of day or night was that,

14   please sir?

15 A. It was approximately 9:44 a.m. when I arrived.

16 Q. Do you know whose residence that was?

17 A. It was the residence of Mrs. Ida Davison.

18 Q. Did you know Mrs. Ida C. Davison?

19 A. Yes, sir, I did.

20 Q. How long had you known Mrs. Davison?

21 A. Approximately twenty years.

22 Q. Now, upon your arrival at the Davison residence, who,

23   if anyone, accompanied you, sir?

24 A. Officer Richard Henry.

25 Q. And he is also an officer with the Texas City Police

1 Department?

2 A. Yes, sir, he is.

3 Q. Upon your arrival at the residence, sir, where did you
4   go?

5 A. Went to the south side of the house, or to the back
6   yard- first of all.

7 Q. Upon entering the back yard- after you went to the
8   back yard, where did you go?

9 A. Entered the house.

10 Q. I take it then, sir, that you entered through the
11   kitchen area?

12 A. That's right.

13 Q. Did you see anything unusual upon entrance into the
14   kitchen?

15 A. Yes, I did.

16 Q. What was that?

17 A. Saw Mrs. Davison lying on the kitchen floor.

18 Q. And how was she lying on the floor, if you recall,
19   Mr. Oliver?

20 A. She was lying on her back- her head was to the south
21   or nearest the kitchen door that we had entered. Her
22   feet were to the north, spread apart. Her hands were
23   to her side. There was a large amount of blood on the
24   floor, and on her head- and she was bleeding severely-
25   profusely. Some wounds were on her head. She was also

1   bleeding from the vaginal area.

2 Q. How was her clothing arrayed, if you recall?

3 A. Yes, sir- her clothing was- her housecoat and gown

4   or slip, was pulled- up above- up to her waist-

5   exposing the lower half of her body.

6 Q. Now, you say that there was blood coming from the

7   vaginal area?

8 A. Yes, sir, there was.

9 Q. Was she alive at that time, sir?

10 A. Yes, sir, she was.

11 Q. Were you present when she was removed from the scene?

12 A. Yes, sir, I was.

13 Q. And by whom was she removed?

14 A. By Crowder ambulance.

15 Q. Do you know where she was taken?

16 A. Taken to County Memorial Hospital.

17 Q. Upon the body- upon the person, rather, of Mrs.

18   Davison being removed, did you then conduct an examin-

19   ation of the area in the vicinity of where she had

20   been laying?

21 A. Yes, sir, we did.

22 Q. Did you note anything unusual there?

23 A. Yes, sir.

24 Q. What was that?

25 A. There was a tooth on the floor, beneath where her head

1		was.
2	Q.	Did you later have occasion to go to County Memorial
3		Hospital?
4	A.	Yes, sir, I did.
5	Q.	And what time did you go there- to the hospital?
6	A.	The ambulance left, and I left approximately ten
7		minutes later.
8	Q.	I will ask you whether or not Chief of Police Rankin
9		DeWalt and Sergeant Saragosa of the Texas City Police
10		Department arrived at the residence?
11	A.	Yes, they arrived at the scene.
12	Q.	And how long did you remain at the County Memorial
13		Hospital, Mr. Oliver?
14	A.	Until she passed away.
15	Q.	Were you there when she died?
16	A.	Yes, I was.
17	Q.	And about what time was that?
18	A.	Approximately twelve noon.
19	Q.	And that's on the 19th day of September?
20	A.	Yes, sir.
21	Q.	I direct your attention to the man seated at the
22		opposite end of the table- opposite me- at the other
23		end- do you know him?
24	A.	Yes, sir.
25	Q.	Did you have occasion to see him on or about the 19th

175

1   day of September, 1970?

2   A. Yes, I did.

3   Q. Where was that, sir?

4   A. At the police station.

5   Q. What time of day or night did you see him at the

6   police station?

7   A. Approximately, 5:17 p.m. on the 19th.

8   Q. And in whose company was he, at the police station,

9   as you recall?

10   A. He was brought in by Officer Eden and Officer Monroe,

11   of the Texas City Police Department.

12   Q. Did you notice anything unusual about his physical

13   appearance, at that time?

14   A. Yes, sir.

15   Q. What was that, sir?

16   A. The clothing he was wearing.

17   Q. And what was unusual about the clothing?

18   A. The shirt had what appeared to be bloodstains.

19   Q. Did you later take possession of his clothing?

20   A. Yes, sir, I did.

21   Q. Now, I will ask you whether or not Judge Ted Bishop,

22   Justice of the Peace in Texas City, had occasion to

23   come to the Texas City police station?

24   A. Yes, sir, he did.

25   Q. When was that, Officer?

1	A.	Approximately, 6:30 p.m. on the 19th.
2	Q.	What, if anything, did Judge Bishop do upon his
3		arrival?
4	A.	He advised Avie of his rights.
5	Q.	Were you present when he advised him of his rights?
6	A.	Yes, sir, I was.
7	Q.	And did you later have a conversation with Johnnie
8		Avie?
9	A.	Yes, sir, I did.
10	Q.	As a result of that conversation, did he give you any
11		sort of a statement?
12	A.	Yes, sir, he did.
13	Q.	And before taking a statement, did you give him any
14		sort of a warning?
15	A.	Yes, sir, I did.
16	Q.	Was that statement reduced to writing?
17	A.	Yes, sir, it was.
18	Q.	And when did he give you this statement, sir?
19	A.	At approximately 8:40 p.m.
20	Q.	And that was on what date?
21	A.	Nineteenth.
22	Q.	Did you have a conversation with him at a later date?
23	A.	Yes, sir, I did.
24	Q.	Did you, at that time, take a statement from him?
25	A.	Yes, sir, I did.

1	Q.	Did you reduce that statement to writing?
2	A.	Yes, sir, I did.
3	Q.	Did he sign that statement?
4	A.	Yes, sir, he did.
5	Q.	And before he placed his signature on that statement,
6		did you again warn him?
7	A.	Yes, sir, I did.
8	Q.	Did you have occasion to see Judge Bishop again,
9		at the Texas City Police Station?
10	A.	Yes, sir, I did.
11	Q.	And when was that, Mr. Oliver?
12	A.	At approximately 10:10 p.m. on the 19th.
13	Q.	And what was his purpose in being there at that time?
14	A.	To accept formal charges.
15	Q.	And formal charges- what charges were filed, if any?
16	A.	Murder.
17	Q.	Was he again- did he again advise the Defendant,
18		Johnnie Avie, of his rights?
19	A.	Yes, sir, he did.
20	Q.	Mr. Oliver, did you have occasion to converse with
21		the Defendant, Johnnie Avie, on the 20th day of
22		September, 1970?
23	A.	Yes, I did.
24	Q.	And as a result of that conversation, did he give you
25		a statement then?

1   A. Yes, he did.

2   Q. Did you reduce that statement to writing?

3   A. Yes, sir.

4   Q. Before he signed it- or I will ask you, did he sign it?

5   A. Yes, sir.

6   Q. And did you- before he signed it- warn him of his
7   rights?

8   A. Yes, sir, I did.

9   Q. Have you brought that statement with you?

10 A. Yes, sir.

11 Q. Will you produce it, please- (Witness hands paper to
12   Mr. Damiani).

13   Mr. Reporter, would you mark this as State's
14   Exhibit 2 for identification, please sir. (Statement
15   is marked S-2).

16   And this is State's Exhibit 2A for identification
17   and I ask you to so mark it, please, sir- (Instrument
18   is marked S-2A, initialed Ray O'N, and dated 10/23/70).

19   Officer Oliver, I show you what has been marked
20   as State's Exhibit 2 for identification, and ask you
21   what that purports to be?

22 A. This is the voluntary statement that I took from Avie,
23   at 12:05 o'clock p.m., on the 20th day of September,
24   1970.

25 Q. I show you, sir, what has been marked as State's

1   Exhibit 2A for identification, and ask you what that

2   purports to be?

3 A. This is the same statement- copy of the original

4   statement.

5 Q. All right, sir. And you are testifying now that this

6   2A for identification, is a photostatic copy of

7   State's Exhibit 2 for identification?

8 A. Yes, sir, it is.

9 COURT:

10   All right, sir- they are identical, are they?

11 A. Yes, sir, they are.

12 MR. DAMIANI:

13   At this time, Your Honor, the State would introduce

14   into evidence State's Exhibit 2A for identification,

15   as State's Exhibit 2A- (Mr. Allmond examines this

16   instrument).

17 COURT:

18   Is there any objection to the introduction of State's

19   Exhibit 2A?

20 MR. ALLMOND:

21   There is, Your Honor- there are objections on the

22   following grounds, Your Honor: That there has been

23   no showing that Deril Oliver advised the Defendant

24   that he had a right to have a lawyer present- to

25   advise him, either prior to any beginning or during

180

1   I mean, prior to any questioning or during any
2   questioning. Further, there has been no showing
3   that Deril Oliver advised the Defendant that if he
4   was unable to employ a lawyer to represent him, that
5   he had a right to have a lawyer appointed to counsel
6   with him prior to any questioning, or to be with him
7   while questioning. Further, there has been no
8   showing that Deril Oliver advised the Defendant that
9   he had a right to remain silent and not make any
10 statements at all, and that any statement he might
11 make could be used in evidence in the trial against
12 him. And, further, that there has been no showing
13 that the Defendant knowingly, intelligently, and
14 voluntarily waived these rights prior to making any
15 statement. These are the requisites of a confession
16 under Article 38.22 of the Code of Criminal Procedure
17 for the State of Texas, and there be no proper
18 showing- correction- there would be no proper predicate
19 laid by showing that the Statute has been complied with-
20 therefore, the Defendant objects to the introduction
21 of this confession.
22 COURT:
23   Mr. Damiani.
24 MR. DAMIANI:
25   I will take him back, Your Honor, and re-introduce it.

COURT:

    All right.

MR. DAMIANI:

    Mr. Oliver, you testified, sir, that you advised
    Johnnie Avie of his rights, before you took a
    statement?

A. Yes, sir, I did.

Q. Sir, I will ask you whether or not you did advise him
    of his rights in accordance with the printed portion
    of the upper portion of State's Exhibit 2A for
    identification.

A. Yes, sir, I did.

Q. Read that into the record.

A. Beginning at the top- Voluntary Statement--

MR. ALLMOND:

    Your Honor, I object to the witness reading from
    the very document that I am trying to keep out of
    evidence. I have made an objection to the introduction,
    and it has not been introduced into evidence, and I
    don't believe that any part of it should be read to
    the Court.

COURT:

    That objection is overruled.

MR. ALLMOND:

    Note our exception.

1 MR. DAMIANI:

2   Just the portion, if any, which you read to him—

3   before he signed the confession.

4 A. Yes, sir.

5   "I, Johnny Avie, before being interrogated

6   and after first--"

7 COURT:

8   Sir, I don't believe that answers the question.

9 MR. DAMIANI:

10   No, sir.

11   Just what warning that you gave to him, Mr.

12   Oliver. In other words, did you give him--

13 A. This section here- (Witness points to location on

14   instrument marked S-2A).

15 Q. Yes, sir.

16 A. That I have the right--

17 COURT:

18   Let Mr. Damiani finish his question.

19 MR. DAMIANI:

20   Did you give him any of the warning contained in the

21   upper portion of this particular instrument?

22 A. Yes, sir, I did.

23 Q. And what portion- what warning, if any, contained

24   therein, did you give him?

25 A. This area right here- (Witness indicates by pointing

183

1   to location on instrument held by Mr. Damiani).

2   Q. All right. Would you read that into the record,

3   please, sir?

4   A. Yes, sir. (Witness then reads from the instrument

5   offered as follows:

6   "That I have a right to retain counsel; that

7   I have a right to remain silent; that I have a right

8   to have an attorney present during any interview with

9   peace officers or attorneys representing the State;

10   that I have the right to terminate the interview at

11   any time; that if I am unable to afford and obtain

12   counsel, that I have the right to request the appoint-

13   ment of counsel; that I have the right to have an

14   examining trial; that I am not required to make any

15   statement at all, and that any statement I do make,

16   may be used against me."

17   Q. And did you read that and explain that to the

18   Defendant, Johnnie Avie?

19   A. Yes, sir.

20   Q. Did he seem to understand it?

21   A. Yes, sir.

22   Q. After you read that statement, did he read that

23   statement- himself?

24   A. Yes, sir, he did.

25   Q. Did he then sign the statement?

184

1   A.   Yes, sir, he did.

2   Q.   All right, sir. At this time, Your Honor, the State

3   introduces into evidence State's Exhibit 2A for

4   identification as State's Exhibit 2A.

5   COURT:

6   All right. Is there any objection?

7   MR. ALLMOND:

8   Your Honor, I would like to take the witness on voir

9   dire.

10   COURT:

11   All right, sir.

12

13   ON VOIR DIRE EXAMINATION BY MR. ALLMOND:

14

15   Q.   Now, sir, what time did you take this Exhibit 2A—

16   this so-called statement from the Defendant?

17   A.   At approximately 12:05 p.m. on the 20th.

18   Q.   On the 20th?

19   A.   Yes, sir.

20   Q.   Of September?

21   A.   Yes, sir.

22   Q.   All right. Now, when did you first see the Defendant—

23   Johnnie Avie?

24   A.   At approximately 5:17 p.m. on the 19th.

25   Q.   5:17 p.m. on the 19th?

185

1	A. Yes, sir.
2	Q. And when you first saw him, he was in the Texas City
3	police station?
4	A. Yes, sir, that's correct.
5	Q. And do you know, of your own knowledge, how long he
6	had been there?
7	A. I saw him there- as soon as he walked in the door.
8	Q. In other words, at 5:19 on the 19th, he came in?
9	A. He was brought into the police station at approximately
10	5:17 p.m., and I was at the station when he was brought
11	in, and I saw him when he was brought in.
12	Q. All right. Now, do you know where he was between
13	5:19 p.m. on the 19th and at 12 o'clock on the 20th,
14	when he made this statement?
15	A. Yes, sir.
16	Q. Were you with him during any of that time?
17	A. Yes, sir.
18	Q. Where were you with him?
19	A. I was at the police station.
20	Q. And were you in the Chief of Police's office or cell
21	or where were you?
22	A. It was in my office.
23	Q. And during that time you were questioning the Defendant
24	is that correct?
25	A. Part of the time- yes, sir.

186

1   Q.   Other parts of the time, the Defendant, when he wasn't

2   being questioned, he was in his cell?

3   A.   Most of the time.

4   Q.   Did you leave the police station that night?

5   A.   Yes, sir.

6   Q.   What time did you leave?

7   A.   Approximately 11 p.m.

8   Q.   On the night of the 19th?

9   A.   19th- yes, sir.

10   Q.   And did you talk to the Defendant just prior to

11   leaving?

12   A.   The last time I talked to him was at approximately-

13   approximately, 10:25 p.m. on the 19th of September.

14   Q.   All right. And who was with him when you left his

15   presence?

16   A.   He was confined to his cell.

17   Q.   All right. When did you see him the next morning?

18   A.   Approximately, 11 a.m.

19   Q.   When you first saw him- when you first saw the

20   Defendant on the afternoon of the 19th, at the

21   police station, did you consider that there was

22   anything unusual about his demeanor, or his behavior?

23   A.   No.

24   Q.   Do you have an opinion as to whether he was intoxicated

25   or under the influence of any sort of narcotic drug?

187

1	A.	He didn't appear to be- intoxicated.
2	Q.	Do you know when he had been arrested?
3	A.	Approximately two or three minutes prior to the time
4		I saw him.
5	Q.	And who were the officers that made the arrest?
6	A.	Officer Eden and Officer Monroe.
7	Q.	Are they both with the Texas City Police Department?
8	A.	Yes, sir, they are.
9	Q.	Now, in regard to the warning of the rights that you
10		say you gave this Defendant prior to the time he signed
11		this confession, what did you tell the Defendant?
12	A.	I advised him of his rights.
13	Q.	How did you advise him- what did you tell him?
14	A.	The same thing that I told him up here- this was read
15		to him before he signed it, and then I had him to
16		read it before he signed it, and then, I had him sign
17		a waiver of rights form on the previous day, which was
18		also read to him, and he also read it himself- him
19		signing the statement that he did understand it.
20	Q.	Was the source of the warning that you gave him, taken
21		from that document there which you have before you?
22	A.	This one, sir- (Witness indicates instrument that had
23		been marked S-2A, entitled Voluntary Statement of
24		Johnny Avie").
25	Q.	Right.

1   A. I read the entire statement- the entire body of it to
2   him.
3   Q. You read it to him?
4   A. I read it to him, and then, I gave it to him and he
5   read it- part of it he read out loud, and part of it
6   he did not.
7   Q. Now, did he at any time ask to use a telephone to
8   call anybody?
9   A. No, sir. The telephone was only brought up one time.
10   Q. When was that?
11   A. I asked him if he would like to make a phone call,
12   and he said- no, he would not like to use the phone
13   to make a call, and he would not like to have any
14   visitors.
15   Q. And when was the phone brought up- that one time?
16   A. Prior to retiring on the night of the 19th.
17   Q. And at any time thereafter, was a phone made available
18   to him?
19   A. He was never refused. He had every opportunity to use
20   a phone.
21   Q. Did he request to use the phone?
22   A. No, sir- not to my knowledge.
23   Q. Well, did he ask you?
24   A. He never asked me to use the phone.
25   Q. Did he ever ask to- did he ever ask about any of his

189

1   family?

2 A. No. The only request he made was that he receive no

3   visitors.

4 Q. Did any of his family ever come to the police station

5   to inquire about his whereabouts?

6 A. Not while I was present. I understand that they did,

7   and I understand they were allowed to see him.

8 Q. Officer, the warning that you gave the Defendant, was

9   it reading that instrument to him?

10 A. Yes, sir. (Mr. Allmond specifies the instrument he

11   is referring to by showing the witness the paper that

12   had been marked S-2A, styled Voluntary Statement of

13   Johnny Avie).

14 Q. Your Honor- I object to the introduction on the

15   grounds that the officer's own testimony is, and he

16   so testified earlier in the questioning by Mr. Damiani,

17   was- that what was told to the Defendant was-"that I

18   have a right to retain counsel; that I have a right

19   to remain silent; that I have a right to have an

20   attorney present during any interview with peace

21   officers, or attorneys representing the State; that I

22   have the right to terminate the interview at any time;

23   that if I am unable to afford and obtain counsel, I

24   have the right to request the appointment of counsel;

25   that I have the right to have an examining trial, that

1 I'm not required to make any statement at all, and
2 that any statement I do make may be used against me."
3 Your Honor, the form in which this warning was
4 given, was given in the nominative singular- in that
5 he is standing there telling the man that he- that I
6 have the right to have an attorney. Well, this is not
7 what we are looking at. What we are looking at- did
8 he, tell Johnnie Avie, that you, Johnnie Avie- that
9 you have the right to have an attorney. That you have
10 the right to make a telephone call, and whether or not
11 Deril Oliver is telling Johnnie Avie that I, Deril
12 Oliver, have a right to obtain counsel, and I have
13 the right to terminate an interview any time I want
14 to- does not comport, Your Honor, with an intelligent
15 conveyance to the Defendant of what his actual rights
16 are, under Article 3822. That the mere reading of a
17 warning in nominative singular, whereby Deril Oliver
18 is explaining to some defendant what Deril Oliver's
19 rights may be, does not then meet the statutory
20 requirement that Johnnie Avie intelligently and
21 knowingly is told that Johnnie Avie has the right to
22 do these things- you have the right, and not Deril
23 Oliver, and the statutory language- Your Honor,
24 says that. It does not say that the Defendant has
25 to be told that the interrogating officer has these

At this point there was one page missing in the transcript files that I was unable to acquire.

191

1   MR. DAMIANI:

2   You pass the witness?

3   MR. ALLMOND:

4   I pass the witness.

5

6

7   DIRECT EXAMINATION BY MR. DAMIANI - RESUMED:

8

9   Q.   Mr. Oliver, when I asked you what warning, if any,

10   you gave to the Defendant, and you read from that

11   instrument- there- you read as it shows on the head

12   of the instrument there- is that correct- on the top

13   portion?

14   A.   Yes, sir.

15   Q.   Now, did you tell Johnnie Avie that he had these

16   rights?

17   A.   Yes, sir, I did.

18   Q.   And he had previously been warned by the Justice of

19   the Peace- is that correct?

20   A.   That's correct, sir.

21   Q.   Do you have that warning that was given by the Justice

22   of the Peace- do you have that too?

23   A.   Yes, sir, I do.

24   Q.   Will you produce it, please- (Witness hands paper to

25   Mr. Damiani).

At this point there was one page missing in the transcript files that I was unable to acquire.

192

hearsay- that further, there is no- of course, the
Court has overruled my objection on the basis it is
hearsay, but I further object on the grounds there is
no evidence here that the signature which appears on
the purported warning is that of the Magistrate.
There is no proof that the name that appears on here
is that of Ted Bishop or of any other magistrate. We
further object, Your Honor, on the grounds that at the
time at which the alleged warning was given, as stated
in the Exhibit, would be many, many hours prior to the
time that the State's Exhibit 2A, which has been
offered, was given. On this basis, we object to the
present State's Exhibit being introduced.

COURT:

May I see it, please- (Instrument marked S-3 is handed
to the Court).

Mr. Oliver- as I understand it, you have
testified that you were present when this warning was
given?

A. Yes, sir, I was.

Q. Do you recall Judge Bishop signing this at that time?

A. Yes, sir, he did.

Q. All right. The objection is overruled, and State's
Exhibit 3 is admitted- (State's Exhibit 3 appears
herein, attached to the following page:)

At this point there was one page missing in the transcript files that I was unable to acquire.

MR. ALLMOND:

Your Honor, I want my exception to the Court's ruling

admitting State's Exhibit 3 into evidence.

COURT:

All right. You may have your objection.

MR. DAMIANI:

Your Honor, we again reurge at this time, the intro-

duction of State's Exhibit 2A for identification, into

evidence as State's Exhibit 2A for the reason that the

Statues only contemplate that one warning be given-

Harris vs. State is authority for that- that it was not

even necessary to get a bench warrant by the magistrate-

no need for further warning, when he has been warned

by the magistrate.

COURT:

All right. The objection is overruled. State's

Exhibit 2A may be admitted.

MR. DAMIANI:

May I read it into the record?

COURT:

Are you going to read it word for word?

MR. DAMIANI:

Yes, Your Honor.

COURT:

All right. Then, there will be no need for the

1   Reporter to take it down, and you can read it more

2   rapidly.

3   MR. DAMIANI:

4   Yes, sir. Thank you- (Reporter's Note: Exhibit

5   marked S-2A appears herein, attached to page 40$ is

6   read).

7   I pass the witness, Your Honor.

8

9

10   ON CROSS EXAMINATION BY MR. ALLMOND:

11

12   Q. Mr. Oliver, do you know who actually made the arrest

13   of the Defendant- Johnnie Avie?

14   A. Officer Eden.

15   Q. And--

16   A. Officer Eden and Officer Monroe brought him in, at

17   5:17 p.m.

18   Q. Do you know how they happened to have occasion to

19   arrest him?

20   A. They saw him downtown, on a public street, and we had

21   some old traffic form of municipal court, and also we

22   wanted to talk to him in reference to this.

23   Q. For old traffic tickets with warrants?

24   A. Yes, sir.

25   Q. And for what reason did he want to talk to him, about

1   this particular crime?

2 A. Due to circumstances on the morning of the 19th of

3   September, where he was seen in the vicinity, acting

4   in a strange and unusual manner.

5 Q. Would you tell us what this strange or unusual manner

6   was?

7 A. He was seen at the I. C. Fish Market, and was reported

8   by the owner and operator, as being present and trying

9   to get into her store, and the person was acting very

10   strangely- was reported to us as acting very strange,

11   and--

12 Q. By strange, did she mean intoxicated or insane or

13   something of that manner?

14 A. Yes, sir- evidently so.

15 Q. As a person not having their normal faculties?

16 A. Right.

17 MR. DAMIANI:

18   Your Honor, that would call for the rankest conclusion

19   on the part of this officer.

20 COURT:

21   Well, you let him answer all these other questions-

22   what other people were thinking, I don't know how he

23   could know. Objection is sustained.

24 MR. ALIMOND:

25   Now, did you find anything, at any time, or do you

1   know of anything that was found on the person of

2   Johnnie Avie, that came from the residence of the

3   deceased?

4 A. Anything that actually came from the residence?

5 Q. Yes, sir.

6 A. Not to my knowledge.

7 Q. Do you know of any fingerprints that were taken at

8   the residence of the deceased?

9 A. Lt. Saragosa did test for latent fingerprints.

10 Q. Do you know whether or not he took any prints?

11 A. It's my understanding that he did.

12 Q. Do you know whether or not he made any comparison?

13 A. Yes, sir, he did.

14 Q. Do you know whether or not those were the prints of

15   Johnnie Avie, as far as your opinion goes?

16 A. It's my understanding they were.

17 Q. Do you know of any person that allegedly saw the

18   Defendant leave the scene of the deceased's home?

19 A. No, sir.

20 Q. You say that when you saw him at the police station,

21   he had blood- or a bloodlike appearing substance on

22   his clothing?

23 A. Yes, sir.

24 Q. But, at the time you saw him at the police station,

25   it is your testimony that there was not anything

```
 1        peculiar about his behavior- is that right?
 2   A.   Nothing at all.
 3   Q.   He seemed perfectly normal to you?
 4   A.   Yes, sir.
 5   Q.   Did you have a conversation with him immediately at
 6        the point of his arrival at the police station?
 7   A.   No, sir.
 8   Q.   How long was it after he did arrive, that you did
 9        have a conversation with him.
10   A.   He arrived at approximately 5:17 p.m., and my first
11        conversation with him was at approximately 6:35 p.m.
12   Q.   At the time that this warning was allegedly given by
13        Judge Bishop to the Defendant, did Judge Bishop read
14        these questions all in sequence, or did he read them
15        one at a time and ask for a response?
16   A.   He read the entire warning, and then he asked if he
17        understood, and I believe he made a notation that the
18        person did state that he understood.
19   Q.   On the various portions of the warning, after asking
20        a question- do you understand that you have the right
21        to remain silent- did he then ask for a response from
22        the Defendant, or did he go on to the next question?
23        Do you understand my thinking- did he say- do you
24        understand you have a right to an attorney and so on,
25        and then ask him did he understand the same?
```

198

```
1   A.  He just went from one to the other- read it slow and
2       precise and loud, where the man could be sure to hear
3       him.
4   Q.  And would he, after he read all of the substance of
5       the warning- then ask him did he understand the same?
6   A.  Yes, sir, he asked him if he understood and had any
7       questions.
8   Q.  You didn't ask him, for instance- did he say- you
9       have the right to remain silent- he, at that time,
10      didn't call for the response of the Defendant- he just
11      went on to the next writing, and then the next one,
12      and asked for--
13  A.  He would hesitate a brief period between each one.
14      I guess he was giving him an opportunity to say some-
15      thing, if he wanted to say anything.
16  Q.  Did you ever hear the Defendant make any response at
17      all to any of these things?
18  A.  Except that he did understand them.
19  Q.  Well, what did he say?
20  A.  The Judge asked him, do you understand what I have
21      read to you, and he said- yes, sir. He said- do you
22      have any questions- I forget the exact statement, but
23      mainly he said- no, sir.
24  Q.  Now, earlier you said there was a telephone brought
25      in at some period here- at what time was the telephone
```

At this point there was one page missing in the transcript files that I was unable to acquire.

1 Q. Where are they?

2 A. I have them with me.

3 Q. May I see them?

4 A. If Mr. Damiani--

5 MR. DAMIANI:

6   Your Honor, that's proper for Bill of Discovery- we

7   haven't offered anything.

8 COURT:

9   Well, he is entitled to see them. It might save time,

10   right now.

11 MR. DAMIANI:

12   You can show them to him, if he wants to see them-

13   (Instruments are handed to Mr. Allmond, and Mr.

14   Allmond examines same).

15 A. I have the original and also have photostats- are

16   photostats all right?

17 MR. ALLMOND:

18   Yes- (Mr. Allmond takes papers from witness and is

19   reading same).

20   I pass the witness.

21 MR. DAMIANI:

22   I have no further questions of this witness, Your Honor-

23   (Witness is excused by the Court).

24 COURT:

25   All right. Who is the next witness?

MR. DAMIANI:

State rests, Your Honor.

MR. ALLMOND:

Relator rests, Your Honor.

COURT:

All right. I believe that there is no need of taking down the oral argument. I believe the applicant or relator- whatever you want to call it- the Defendant has the right to open and close- (Attorneys for the Defendant and for the State make argument before the Court. Following the argument, the following occurs:)

COURT: Johnnie Avie, would you stand up- (Johnnie Avie does stand). Mr. Damiani, would you go over and stand by him there.

MR. DAMIANI:

Yes, sir. (Mr. Damiani walks over and stands by the Defendant).

COURT:

How tall are you, Mr. Damiani?

MR. DAMIANI:

Five feet, six and a half inches, Your Honor.

COURT:

He is a good foot taller than you are. He must be about six feet six inches, anyway. He looks like he is in the prime of life, and the deceased was an approximately

1 seventy-five year old lady- the lady he killed. Alright-

2 thank you. I believe that the proof is evident that

3 Johnnie Avie, with cool and deliberate mind and formed

4 design, maliciously killed Ida C. Davison, and that upon

5 a hearing of the facts before the Court, a dispassionate

6 Jury would, upon such evidence, not only convict him, but

7 would assess the death penalty.

8   The application for writ of habeas corpus is denied

9 and the applicant, Johnnie Avie, is remanded to the custody

10 of the Sheriff of Galveston County, Texas

11   - - -

12   END OF HEARING
                    - - -

13

14 CERTIFICATE TO FOREGOING TRANSCRIPT OF TESTIMONY:

15

16 THE STATE OF TEXAS

17 COUNTY OF GALVESTON

18   I, Ray O'Neill, Official Court

19 Reporter, Tenth Judicial District, Galveston County, Texas,

20 do hereby certify that I took down in shorthand, to the

21 best of my skill and ability, all of the proceedings had

22 upon Hearing On Application For Writ of Habeas Corpus,

23 had in the above styled and numbered cause and that I

24 later transcribed the same and that the above and foregoing

25 fifty pages hereof constitute a true and correct transcript

    of same.

        Witness my hand this the 7th day of November, 1970.

                    Ray O'Neill, Official Court
                    Reporter, Tenth Judicial District
                    Galveston County, Texas.

Murder File: Actual Court Transcripts From Habeas Corpus Hearing

There is an interesting quote that we can take from the conclusion of this court hearing. A quote made by Judge Markle. He is on record as saying, in reference to Johnnie Avie, "He looks like he is in the prime of life, and the deceased was an approximately seventy-five-year-old lady – the lady he killed." The interesting portion of that quote are the words "*the lady he killed*". But why is that interesting?

In the court of law, an individual is supposed to be innocent until proven guilty. And at the time the hearing took place, Avie was not yet convicted of the murder. So, the judge should not have used language that expressly referred to the victim as being killed by Avie. He should have said something like, "The lady he is accused of killing". It shows that in the minds of many, even officials in the courts, Johnnie Avie was considered to be guilty even before he had his day in court.

At any rate, the Honorable Judge Donald M. Markle denied the writ of Habeas Corpus, and he went on to say that he believed any jury would find that Avie was guilty of this crime and that same jury would see the death penalty as a suitable punishment for him. This decision was a crushing blow to the defense team. Now that it was guaranteed that the confession Avie gave would be admissible in court, it was almost guaranteed that he would be found guilty.

At the conclusion of this hearing, a defeated Avie was transferred back to his jail cell, and all he could do was wait for the courts to give him a trial date. His defense lawyer had no more tricks up his sleeve.

Chapter 11

Avie Pleads Guilty And Gets Sentenced To Life In Prison

After being arrested, charged with Murder with Malice, locked away inside of the Galveston County Jail, denied the right to have his confession withheld from the evidence pool, and told by the Criminal District Attorney that the state of Texas would be seeking the death penalty if he was convicted, Johnnie Avie maintained his innocence and held on to his plea of not guilty. He held this position for almost two full years while he waited on his day in court to arrive.

It is a common saying that people have a right to a speedy trial, but in almost all cases, an individual must spend years in jail before they get the opportunity to have their case tried at trial. In Texas, so many people get locked up, that the entire court system exists in a perpetual state of being backed up. Why? Simply because it takes time for the state to prepare for a trial. It takes time and also money.

So, imagine for a second that one person gets arrested, and they decide to get their case heard before a jury of their peers. But, before their trial date comes, 20 more people get arrested and those 20 people also want to have their case heard before a jury of their peers. Now, the state has to prepare for 21 trial cases. The truth is, the number of prosecutors for the state is limited, the number of judges is limited, and the number of people who can and will serve as jurors is limited.

This means, by the time the state is ready to take those 21 people to trial, another 100 people will need trial dates set because more and more people will be arrested while the state prepares to try the people who have already been arrested. Before the state will be ready to try those 100 more people, they will have another 2,100 trials to prepare for. Unfortunately for them, there are only 365 days in a year, and almost all trials last longer than one day. If we would simply view this as a mathematical formula, we would quickly realize that it is impossible for the state to take every single inmate in jail to trial.

To solve this problem, the courts devised a system of accepting plea deals. They tell the prisoners that if they simply waive their right to a speedy trial and admit they are guilty of the crime they are accused of, then the state will give them a deal. Perhaps the crime you committed holds a prison sentence of 2 – 20 years. The prosecutor will tell you that if you waive your rights to go to trial and just plead guilty, then they will only give you 2 years in prison. That way you do not have to risk getting 20 years if you are found guilty at trial.

The vast majority of criminals, when they hear this, take the deal. They simply admit their guilt as opposed to risking going to trial and getting sentenced to 20 years in prison. The state will also give the people who refuse to take the plea deal an exorbitant amount of time in order to deter other prisoners from going to trial. Why? Because the state cannot take all of the prisoners to trial. It is logistically impossible. However, the prisoners who refuse the plea deal still must wait for several years before they get their day in court, because the system is still backed up.

Johnnie Avie fell into this category. Honestly, I'm not sure if they even offered him a plea deal in the beginning. The only records I have seen stated that the district attorney wanted him to get the death penalty. Subsequently, he sat inside of the Galveston County Jail from September 21, 1970, until February 8, 1972, before the state was finally ready to take him to trial. In February of 1972, the process of selecting the 12 jurors that would hear the case began. By this time, Avie's original lawyer was out of the picture, and he was now being represented by a man named Tom Douvry.

Tom Douvry was a former first assistant district attorney who was now in the private practice of law. I am not sure why Johnnie Avie's first lawyer was no longer representing him, but it is possible that Avie could not pay his fees. With his new lawyer being a former assistant to the district attorney, that could go one of two ways for Avie. Either it was a good thing because Tom Douvry knew how the district attorney's office operated and he could more easily navigate through the trial, or he was still loyal to people within the district attorney's   office, and he was willing to sell Avie out to gain favor.

Whatever his true intentions were, this was the defense lawyer Avie had. On February 8, 1972, the two sides met in the 56th District Court before Judge Hugh Gibson. The purpose of this court proceeding was to begin the process of selecting a jury of 12 people who would decide Avie's fate. The defense's main objective was to select jurors that were capable of sentencing a person to probation for a first offense. Even though Avie had been arrested plenty of times before, this was his first adult felony charge. In the event that the jury found him guilty, the defense wanted members of the juror that would consider probation as a punishment instead of the death penalty.

In all, 10 potential jurors were brought in one by one and quizzed by both the defense and the prosecution. Out of those 10 potential jurors, only 1 juror was agreed upon and selected. There were a number of reasons either the defense or the prosecution could reject a juror, and they utilized these reasons with 5 of the potential jurors. With 4 of the jurors who were rejected, the prosecution and the defense utilized a rule that allowed them to challenge and exempt a potential juror without citing the reason why they were exempting them.

Whenever a capital case is being tried, each side has 15 peremptory challenges where they can reject a juror without assigning a reason. A capital case is a case where the defendant is being charged with a crime so severe that they can be sentenced to death if convicted. This matched the Avie trial because District Attorney Jules Damiani had already ensured that the crime was a capital offense when he made his push for the death penalty.

During the juror selection, the defense used 2 of their 15 challenges and the prosecution used 2 of their 15 challenges. This meant that out of the 10 potential jurors questioned, only 1 was actually selected. Even though this took place almost two years after the brutal murder of Mrs. Ida Davison occurred, the public was still highly invested in Texas City's Most Infamous Murder. Many people were holding their breaths waiting to see if Avie would actually be convicted, and if so, what his punishment would be. This case was so relevant, the Galveston Daily News reporters were continuing to follow it and reporting to their readers the current events.

Juror In Avie Trial Selected

A single juror was selected Tuesday in the murder trial of Johnnie Avie, 18, of Texas City.

The trial is in Judge Hugh Gibson's 56th District Court.

Criminal District Attorney Jules Damiani is seeking the death penalty for Avie, who is accused of the murder of Mrs. Don C. (Ida) Davison, 75, on Sept. 19, 1970, at her home at 109 3rd Ave. North in Texas City.

Avie is being defended by Tom Douvry, former first assistant district attorney, now in the private practice of law

The defense attorney is qualifying prospective jurors on whether or not they can grant probation on a first offense.

Testimony of Dr. Kurt Weiss, at that time an assistant county medical examiner, at a habeaus corpus hearing in Oct., 1970, brought out that Mrs. Davison died from a fractured skull that was "compatable with a beating by fists." He also testified to extensive contusions and abrasions, and said it appeared she had been raped.

Avie has pleaded not guilty to the murder charge.

The single juror was selected out of 10 veniremen quizzed individually by the state and defense Tuesday.

Each side in a capital case has 15 "peremptory" challenges whereby they can excuse a prospective juror without assigning a reason within the rules of procedure to it.

By the time the court adjourned after 5 p.m. on Tuesday, each side had used two out of the 15 peremptory challenges.

Galveston Daily News February 9, 1972

Juror In Avie Trial Selected

A single juror was selected Tuesday in the murder trial of Johnnie Avie, 18, of Texas City.

The trial is in Judge Hugh Gibson's 56th District Court.

Criminal District Attorney Jules Damiani is seeking the death penalty for Avie, who is accused of the murder of Mrs. Don C. (Ida) Davison, 75, on Sept. 19, 1970, at her home at 109 3rd Ave, North in Texas City.

Avie is being defended by Tom Douvry, former first assistant district attorney, now in the private practice of law.

209

The defense attorney is qualifying prospective jurors on whether or not they can grant probation on a first offense.

Testimony of Dr. Kurt Weiss, at that time an assistant county medical examiner, at a habeas corpus hearing in Oct. 1970, brought out that Mrs. Davison died from a fractured skull that was "compatible with a beating by fists." He also testified to extensive contusions and abrasions, and said it appeared she had been raped.

Avie has pleaded not guilty to the murder charge.

The single juror was selected out of 10 veniremen quizzed individually by the state and defense Tuesday.

Each side in a capital case has 15 "peremptory" challenges whereby they can excuse a prospective juror without assigning a reason within the rules of procedure to it.

By the time the court adjourned after 5 p.m. on Tuesday, each side had used two out of the 15 peremptory challenges.

After the process of selecting a juror had begun, Johnnie Avie, aka Pie, began to feel the walls closing in on him. The juror selection made things vastly more real that his incarceration did. It was at this point that Avie began to consider the possibility that he could actually lose his life for this crime. For almost two years he sat inside of the Galveston County Jail doing what most inmates do. Fighting, eating, playing cards, watching TV, and sleeping. Throughout that time, Avie no doubt had it as easy as an inmate could have it.

Not only was he standing around 6'5, but he was also being tried for murder. That charge alone gave him more jailhouse status than someone sitting in prison for a traffic violation. Plus, he was young enough to have the right amount of energy to give the jail hell. It is a well-known fact that the youngsters cause the most trouble in jail. So much so, that anyone who is older hates to be placed in a pod or cell with someone younger. Given Avie's criminal history beginning at the young age of 14, one can assume that he fit right in with the rambunctious youngsters.

The realization that his trial date was drawing closer and closer, caused something inside of Avie's cool as a cucumber persona to snap. Perhaps it was his instincts of self-preservation. The old fight or flight. Perhaps watching the men and women who would decide if he lived or died be chosen is what finally got to him. Perhaps it was the older men inside the jail with him that convinced him not to gamble with his life by going to trial. Or perhaps it was simply remorse. Maybe Avie thought about Mrs. Ida Davison and finally admitted to himself that what he did was wrong, and he wanted to make it right.

Whatever the real reason, the very next day, Wednesday, February 9, 1972, Johnnie Avie appeared in the exact same court and changed his plea from not guilty to guilty.

In my opinion, I believe this was done out of pure instincts of self-preservation. From the moment Avie was officially charged with the crime of murder, there are no records that I have seen that indicate he was offered any type of plea deal. From 1970 until 1972, it seems like the only option on the table for Avie was the death penalty. So why would he admit guilt in open court and effectively sentence himself to die?

For Avie, it was either plead not guilty and pray for a miracle in court or die by electrocution. However, once the juror selection began, the district attorney gave Avie a little hope. They spoke with his lawyer, Tom Douvry, and said that if Avie would plead guilty to the crime, they would give him life in prison instead of sentencing him to death. This was good news. Why? A life sentence did not necessarily mean Avie would die in prison. Depending on the specifics of his plea deal, he could end up serving 15, 20, or possibly 40 years.

All of which were better than death, especially considering how young Avie was when he was arrested for the crime. He was only 18 years old. So, worst case scenario, he could end up doing 40 years in the penitentiary and get out when he was 58. I believe that all Avie was holding out for was a plea deal that spared him from death row.

When his new defense lawyer, Tom Douvry, told Avie about the plea deal on the table, Avie accepted it without any hesitation. The very next day, after just one juror was selected, Avie stood before Judge Hugh Gibson in the 56th District Court, and admitted to attacking, raping, and murdering the beloved member of the Texas City community, Mrs. Ida Davison. He said that the confession he gave to Officer Deril Oliver was correct, and he admitted to also stealing around $4 worth of coins out of the house.

Imagine that. Mrs. Ida Davison lost her life, and her killer only made off with a meager $4 in coins.

At the sentencing of Avie, Lt. Savas Saragoza of the Texas City Police Department also testified that a palm print was found inside of the home on the stove. He stated that this palm print matched a known palm print of Johnnie Avie that the police had on file. The palm print, however, was not listed as evidence collected in the official reports that I have read. Perhaps this was because they did not need to send the palm print off to a lab to have it tested by a certified technician, while the blood and hair samples needed to be examined by an expert.

Judge Hugh Gibson accepted Avie's guilty plea on behalf of the state of Texas, and Johnnie Avie was sentenced to Life inside of the Texas Department of Corrections. It had taken a total of 508 days after the murder of Mrs. Ida Davison for justice to finally be served, but when the news of justice finally came, the Davison family and the Texas City community sighed a sigh of relief. The newspaper article that ran the next morning made many people cry tears of joy. They were happy that Avie was finally convicted, and they felt that Mrs. Ida could finally rest in peace.

Plea Changed, Avie Gets Life

Johnnie Avie, 18, of Texas City, admitted in court Wednesday that he murdered and raped Mrs. Don C. Davison, 75, on Sept. 19, 1970 — and accepted a life sentence for the crime.

Avie confirmed a confession to the crime given to Texas City Police Sgt. Darrell Oliver.

He was being tried in 56th District Court, had asked for a jury trial, and Criminal Dist. Atty. Jules Damiani was seeking the death penalty.

One juror had been selected during the day Tuesday, and Wednesday morning, Avie, through his attorney, Thomas Douvry, announced he was changing his pleading from not guilty to guilty, and wished immediate imposition of the sentence.

After Avie's plea of guilty, Damiani called Lt. Savas Saragoza of the Texas City Police Department Identification Bureau to the witness stand.

Saragoza testified he found a palm print on a stove in the kitchen of the murdered woman's home, and said the palm print matched a known palm print of Avie.

Avie's confession was that he went into the house to steal money, that he had had barbiturates (three 'Christmas Trees'), that he had smoked two marijuana cigarettes, and that he had beaten and raped Mrs. Davison. While he was searching for money -- he found about $4 in nickels, dimes and quarters — he said, Mrs. Davison began to scream, and he fled the house.

Mrs. Davison died at County Memorial Hospital at noon on the same day as the assault.

Galveston Daily News February 10, 1972

Plea Changed, Avie Gets Life

Johnnie Avie, 18, of Texas City, admitted in court Wednesday that he murdered and raped Mrs. Don C. Davison, 75, on Sept. 19, 1970 – and accepted a life sentence for the crime.

Avie confirmed a confession to the crime given to Texas City Police Sgt. Darrell Oliver.

He was being tried in 56th District Court, had asked for a jury trial, and Damiani was seeking the death penalty.

214

One juror had been selected during the day Tuesday, and Wednesday morning, Avie, through his attorney, Thomas Douvry, announced he was changing his pleading from not guilty to guilty, and wished immediate imposition of the sentence.

After Avie's plea of guilty, Damiani called Lt. Savas Saragoza of the Texas City Police Department Identification Bureau to the witness stand.

Saragoza testified he found a palm print on a stove in the kitchen of the murdered woman's home, and said the palm print matched a known palm print of Avie.

Avie's confession was that he went into the house to steal money, that he had had barbiturates (three 'Christmas Trees'), that he had smoked two marijuana cigarettes, and that he had beaten and raped Mrs. Davison. While he was searching for money – he found about $4 in nickels, dimes, and quarters – he said, Mrs. Davison began to scream, and he fled the house.

Mrs. Davison died at County Memorial Hospital at noon on the same day as the assault.

Chapter 12

Don Davison Sells The Davison Home

In 1972, the same year Johnie Avie was sentenced to life in prison for the murder of Mrs. Ida Davison, citizens of Texas City formed an organization called the Texas City Heritage Association. This organization was formed for the express purpose of purchasing The Davison Home and preserving it as a landmark for the community, as well as preserving other aspects of Texas City history.

It is rumored that after the brutal murder described in this work, Mr. Don C. Davison no longer wished to live inside the home because of what happened inside of it. This seems to be the case because when the Heritage Association was formed, Mr. Don Davison had moved out of the house, and it was unoccupied.

Instead of simply selling the home to a random buyer, however, the power structure within Texas City thought that it would be better to preserve the home as opposed to allowing a different family to begin living in a home with so much Texas City history intrinsically tied to it. After all, it was one of the first homes in Texas City, and it was built by the man who was often called the founder of Texas City. After the Texas City Heritage Association was formed, they almost immediately began a crowd funding campaign to purchase The Davison Home, and once again the most famous home in Texas City was back in the headlines.

TC Heritage Plan Set

NEWS MAINLAND BUREAU

TEXAS CITY — Plans have been initiated to set up a non - profit incorporation to undertake projects for perpetuating the heritage of Texas City. The first project on the agenda will be preservation of the Davison home, one of the city's earliest homesites.

Members of the Texas City Historical Commission met Wednesday night to call a public meeting for 7:30 p.m. Wednesday at city hall to organize the new group.

Charles Little, commission chairman, said the historical group will advise the group and members will participate in projects, but the two organizations will be separate entities.

During next week's meeting, Little will explain the purpose of the proposed organization, and in the interest of maintaining organized proceedings, the commission will be prepared to submit recommendations for a title for the group and for a temporary chairman.

The commission's recommendation for the organization's name would be the

Texas City Heritage Foundation, and the name of Mrs. Merlworth Mabry will be submitted as a nomination for temporary chairman. Also needed will be a vice chairman, secretary, and treasurer, all to be elected.

Elected officers will appoint chairmen for committees to spearhead fund raising, publicity, youth activities, and special projects. A special committee will be formed composed of presidents of all local civic and fraternal organizations.

Preservation of the Davison

home has been a topic of interest in Texas City for several months. Located on the corner of Fifth St. and Third Ave. North, the home is the site of a historical marker because of its rule in Texas City's past.

Frank Davison built the home in 1897. It was the birthplace of the first child born in Texas City, the late Mrs. Jean Paul Jones. During the 1900 storm many residents took refuge in the three - story structure.

Davison played an important part in the development of Texas City. He was the first postmaster, one of the first city commissioners, a member of the first school board, and also opened the first grocery store.

Presently unoccupied, the house is still the property of the Davison family, now headed by Don Davison, a son of the Texas City pioneer. The home was placed on the local realty market, but the Davison family removed it from the market about two months ago to allow a community effort for preservation to begin.

Little told historical

See HERITAGE Page 16A

Schwartz On Budget Board

AUSTIN Tex. (AP) — Lt. Gov. Ben Barnes announced the appointments of Sens. A.R. "Babe" Schwartz of Galveston and Tom Creighton of Mineral Wells to the Legislative Budget Board Wednesday.

Sens. A.M. Aikin, of Paris and William T. Moore of Bryan are also members of the board because of their chairmanships, respectively, of the Senate State Affairs Committee and the Senate Finance Committee.

The budget board, composed of the lieutenant governor, the speaker of the house, and four members each of the Senate and House, studies the requests of state agencies and recommends a budget to the Legislature. The governor also makes a budget recommendation.

Barnes' new appointments take effect immediately and expire in January 1973.

Galveston Daily News July 13, 1972

218

Heritage Plan Is Set In TC

(Continued From Page 1)

commission members Wednesday night that a sale price of $16,500 has been set for the house but said the price is open to negotiation. Other estimates obtained include about $3200 for purchase of all contents including furniture in the home, about $15,000 for complete renovation, and about $4,000 if the house is moved to another location.

When the new organization is formed, contributions can be secured to offer earnest money and establish a firm sale price, and the corporation can decide how to proceed with other details, Little said.

Discussion of a community wide project to preserve the home has centered around a drive asking each resident of the community to contribute $1, which would produce all necessary funds and would involve all segments of the community.

Galveston Daily News July 13, 1972

TC Heritage Plan Set

TEXAS CITY – Plans have been initiated to set up a non-profit incorporation to undertake projects for perpetuating the heritage of Texas City. The first project on

219

the agenda will be preservation of the Davison Home, one of the city's earliest homesites.

Members of the Texas City Historical Commission met Wednesday night to call a public meeting for 7:30 p.m. Wednesday at city hall to organize the new group.

Charles Little, commission chairman, said the historical group will advise the group and members will participate in projects, but the two organizations will be separate entities.

During next week's meeting, Little will explain the purpose of the proposed organization, and in the interest of maintaining organized proceedings, the commission will be prepared to submit recommendations for a title for the group and for temporary chairman.

The commission's recommendation for the organization's name would be the Texas City Heritage Foundation, and the name of Mrs. Meriworth Mabry will be submitted as a nomination for temporary chairman. Also needed will be a vice chairman, secretary, and treasurer, all to be elected.

Elected officers will appoint chairmen for committees to spearhead fund raising, publicity, youth activities, and special projects. A special committee will be formed composed of presidents of all local civic and fraternal organizations.

Preservation of the Davison home has been a topic of interest in Texas City for several months. Located on the corner of First St. and Third Ave. North, the home is the site of a historical marker because of its role in Texas City's past.

Frank Davison built the home in 1897. It was the birthplace of the first child born in Texas City, the late Mrs. Jean Paul Jones. During the 1900 storm many residents took refuge in the three-story structure.

Davison played an important part in the development of Texas City. He was the first postmaster, one of the first city commissioners, a member of the first school board, and also opened the first grocery store.

Presently unoccupied, the house is still the property of the Davison family, now headed by Don Davison, a son of the Texas City pioneer. The home was placed on the local realty market, but the Davison family removed it from the market about two months ago to allow a community effort for preservation to begin.

Little told historical commission members Wednesday night that a sale price of $16,500 has been set for the house but said the price is open to negotiation. Other estimates obtained include about $3200 for purchase of all contents including furniture in the home, about $15,000 for complete renovation, and about $4,000 if the house is moved to another location.

When the new organization is formed, contributions can be secured to offer earnest money and establish a firm sale price, and the corporation can decide how to proceed with other details, Little said.

Discussion of a community wide project to preserve the home has centered around a drive asking each resident of the community to contribute $1, which would produce all *necessary funds and would involve all segments of the community.*

Not surprisingly, the citizens of Texas City agreed with the City Commission about the need to preserve The Davison Home for future generations. The people came through in droves to donate what they could. Many people simply understood the historical relevance of the home, and others saw donating as a way to honor the late Mrs. Ida Davison. In fact, one could reasonably assume that had the murder never took place, the Davison family would've never decided to sell the home, and subsequently, the city could never have acquired it.

The crowd funding lasted for around one year, and the Heritage Association was able to collect most of the funds they needed to execute their plan. They needed to purchase the home, purchase the furniture inside of it, and also restore it to its former glory. The funds that were not donated to the cause were obtained through a bank loan.

The next year, 1973, the Heritage Association was ready to implement its design. They secured a final sale price from Mr. Don C. Davison, purchased the property and the furniture inside of it, then moved into the restoration phase. They also came to an agreement with the City of Texas City that ensured the home would be enjoyed for countless generations to come. The Association deeded the home to the city, and in turn the city would lease the home back to the Association for a minimal yearly fee.

This made the ultimate responsibility of the home rest on the shoulders of Texas City itself. Even if the Heritage Association one day goes away, or even if they go bankrupt, The Davison Home will still be maintained by the one who possesses the deed to the property. And the one who possesses the deed is the City of Texas City. In essence, this means that The Davison Home will exist and be maintained as long as the city exists and is maintained. Those citizens who made these decisions back in the 1970's were indeed visionaries, and their insight and thoughtfulness still benefits citizens of Texas City like me today.

Imagine, all of this took place before I was born, yet I am a beneficiary of their great ideas, resolve, and ability to peer beyond the veil of their present and see my future. Today, The Davison Home is both a monument and a museum, and it is still in the same condition that it was in when Mrs. Ida Davison was murdered there. She was the last Davison woman to walk those hollowed hallways as a resident of the home which now means so much to the City of Texas City.

Chapter 13

Avie Tries To Have His Sentence Commuted

As Texas City tried to move on from the murder, Johnnie Avie had one more trick up his sleeve to try and escape the justice imposed upon him. In prison, the vast majority of people who are convicted of heinous crimes and get sentenced to a lot of time, at some point will try to appeal their case. Whether they know they are guilty or not. Even the ones who know full well that they committed the crimes that they were convicted of try to get a new trial through the appeal process so that they can get out of doing the large prison sentence they were given.

Johnnie Avie, serving a life sentence for murder, was no different. Like many others, after confessing to the crime and pleading guilty, he tried to have his conviction overturned. The reasoning that his new lawyer tried to present was that Avie only pled guilty because he was afraid of being sentenced to death. It was also stated that Avie only confessed to the Texas City Police under a form of duress and he did not actually attack and kill Mrs. Ida Davison.

In August of 1975, 5 years after the murder, Johnnie Avie enlisted the help of a lawyer named Gerson D. Bloom. Mr. Bloom was based out of Galveston, Tx., and he worked for a neighborhood law center at St. Vincent's House. When he was arrested, Avie was living with his parents in

Galveston, so it's possible that his family members sought out Mr. Gerson Bloom on his behalf and asked him to help with Avie's appeal.

Mr. Bloom, realizing that Avie had pled guilty to the crime in open court, knew that his only shot at getting the life sentence changed was to challenge the validity of that guilty plea. His plan was to present Avie as a young black male who was falsely accused of raping and murdering an elderly white woman and then forced by police and prosecutors to confess to the crime or risk being put to death. This defense proposed that Avie pled guilty under a form of duress, and this made his plea invalid.

Mr. Bloom is on record as stating that there was "unjust and undue pressure which motivated Mr. Avie's guilty plea." The primary cause of this pressure was the threat of being sent to death row if convicted. Also, the Davison family was so powerful, Avie was convinced that he would be found guilty whether he was actually guilty or not.

By this time, Jules Damiani was no longer the head prosecutor for Galveston County, and a man named Ron Wilson held that position. Mr. Ron Wilson was clear that he would vehemently oppose any clemency for Avie. In his eyes, Avie was a violent criminal who committed one of the most atrocious crimes in the history of Texas City, and he was not about to let him back out on the streets.

Ron Wilson reminded the courts of the disturbing facts surrounding the case and he pointed out how the evidence against Avie was overwhelming. He also stated that not only did Avie confess to the crime while in police custody, but he also plead guilty of his own accord in open court. All of this, Ron Wilson argued, left no room to doubt that the state had indeed convicted the correct man for the crime.

Gerson D. Bloom attempted to mention that this crime was the first felony Avie had ever been convicted of committing, and even if the guilty sentence could not be changed, perhaps the courts could change the life sentence to a lesser sentence. By this time, Johnnie Avie had been in jail for 5 years, and Gerson Bloom was trying to get him a lesser sentence that would see him released either immediately or within the next few years.

The courts agreed with Criminal District Attorney Ron Wilson, and Avie's appeal was denied. The wounds created by the murder of Mrs. Ida Davison had not gone away, and the courts ruled that Avie had not yet paid his debt to society for taking a life in such a violent manner.

Attempt Made To Commute Admitted Killer's Sentence

Efforts are being made to get a commutation of the life sentence of Johnnie Avie, 21, of Texas City, and Criminal District Attorney Ron Wilson said he will oppose any clemency for Avie.

Avie admitted in 56th District Court in Galveston on Feb. 9, 1972 that he had raped and murdered Mrs. Don C. Davison, 75, in Texas City on Sept. 19, 1970.

He had changed his pleading in court from not guilty to guilty after one juror had been selected.

Jules Damiani, criminal district attorney at the time of the trial, was seeking the death penalty for Avie.

Now Gerson D. Bloom, of the neighborhood law center at St. Vincent's House in Galveston, is seeking commutation of the life sentence, contending that Avie pleaded guilty largely to avoid the death penalty.

He said it was "...both unjust and undue pressure which motivated Mr. Avie's guilty plea. By no means did he enter his plea freely and willingly."

Bloom contends that it is a factor that Avie at the time of his trial had never been convicted of a felony.

Wilson's reply to Bloom was: "This subject (Avie) was convicted of a vicious, premeditated murder of a helpless old lady during the course of a robbery. The proof of his guilt was overwhelming.

"Your suggestion that this dangerous man be placed again in our community is incredible. I am and will remain opposed to any clemency for this subject."

When he confessed to the crime in open court, Avie said he went into Mrs. Davison's home to steal money, that he had had barbiturates (three christmas trees), that he had smoked two marijuana cigarettes and that he had beaten and raped Mrs. Davison.

He said in the courtroom that while he was searching

See COMMUTATION Page 2A

Check These

Other Features

Galveston Daily News August 26, 1975

Commutation Of Sentence Is Attempted

(Continued From Page 1)

for money—he found about $4 in nickels, dimes and quarters—Mrs. Davison began to scream.

She died from a fractured skull received in the beating, according to medical testimony at the time.

Galveston Daily News August 26, 1975

Attempt Made To Commute Admitted Killer's Sentence

Efforts are being made to get a commutation of the life sentence of Johnnie Avie, 21, of Texas City, and Criminal District Attorney Ron Wilson said he will oppose any clemency for Avie.

Avie admitted in 56th District Court in Galveston on Feb. 9, 1972 that he had raped and murdered Mrs. Don C. Davison, 75, in Texas City on Sept. 19, 1970.

He had changed his pleading in court from not guilty after one juror had been selected.

Jules Damiani, criminal district attorney at the time of the trial, was seeking the death penalty for Avie.

Now Gerson D. Bloom, of the neighborhood law center at St. Vincent's House in Galveston, is seeking commutation of the life sentence, contending that Avie pleaded guilty largely to avoid the death penalty.

He said it was "...both unjust and undue pressure which motivated Mr. Avie's guilty plea. By no means did he enter his plea freely and willingly."

Bloom contends that it is a factor that Avie at the time of his trial had never been convicted of a felony.

Wilson's reply to Bloom was: "This subject (Avie) was convicted of a vicious, premeditated murder of a helpless old lady during the course of a robbery. The proof of his guilt was overwhelming.

"Your suggestion that this dangerous man be placed again in our community is incredible. I am and will remain opposed to any clemency for this subject."

When he confessed to the crime in open court, Avie said he went into Mrs. Davison's home to steal money, that he had had barbiturates (three Christmas trees), that he had smoked two marijuana cigarettes and that he had beaten and raped Mrs. Davison.

He said in the courtroom that while he was searching for money – he found about $4 in nickels, dimes and quarters – Mrs. Davison began to scream.

She died from a fractured skull received in the beating, according to medical testimony at the time.

This last-ditch effort made by Johnnie Avie failed, and his life sentence remained. I do not know how many years of his life sentence Avie actually served, but I do know that he did not die in prison. At some point, Johnnie Avie was released from prison, and he had the opportunity to experience life on the outside of a prison cell. According to the official records, Avie contracted cancer and this was the ultimate cause of his death.

At the age of 58, on August 10, 2011, Johnnie Avie, aka Pie, passed away and was laid to rest by family and friends. **(See Photo 1A at the end of this chapter.)** Unfortunately, because of this, I was not able to locate him and interview him about this murder and hear his side of the story. One might say that Avie made the right choice when he took the life sentence instead of risking the death penalty. At least he was able to feel the sunshine upon his skin as a free man one more time before he left his earth.

There are those, however, who think that because Mrs. Ida Davison never had the opportunity to feel the sunshine again after Avie entered her home that fateful morning in 1970, Avie didn't deserve to ever experience freedom again. This author has his own personal feelings about the case, but I will keep my opinions to myself. I will leave it up to you, the reader, to come to your own conclusions and feel however you wish to feel.

Photo 1A

Johnnie Avie Obituary

Chapter 14

The Davison Home Is Now A Museum And Anyone Can Visit

...ning Committee met for two and one-half hours, accomplish-

...versity of Texas Art museum to display a $1 million collection of paintings depicting Texas his-

...structure committees to tackle various sections of the constitution and three procedural com-

Historic Davison Home Open Today For Tours

News Mainland Bureau

TEXAS CITY — The historic Davison home will be open to the public from 2 to 5 p.m. today to allow tours of all three floors of the home.

The Texas City Heritage Association is sponsoring the tour to raise funds to pay off the purchase note on the home and for future restoration. Donations will be $1 for adults and 25 cents for children under 12 years.

Purchase of Texas City's first home has been a community project coordinated by the Heritage Association. The title on the home will be deeded to the City of Texas City so the home can become a city attraction.

The Victorian structure located at Third Ave. North and First St. was built in 1897. Frank Davison, original owner of the home, was among the small group of men who founded the present community of Texas City and was among the town's first businessmen.

SILVER DOLLAR MEDALLIONS WITH CHAIN

Galveston Daily News Oct 28, 1973

The Davison Home still stands as an iconic reminder of Texas City's humble beginnings. It has now been converted into a museum that is open to the public on the first Sunday of each month. Visitors are required to make a donation of $1 when they attend the guided tour. Anyone can attend these tours when they are offered. They are available to both Texas City citizens as well as anyone else who would like to experience this beautiful structure firsthand.

The tour guide is full of information that is not widely known and publicized. They do not speak about the murder of Mrs. Ida Davison during these tours, however. On some level, the story of how Mrs. Ida Davison lost her life has been lost to the citizens of Texas City. Even those who are old enough to know that it happened have no idea about the details I have revealed in this book. As I worked on this book, I began to think that perhaps I was being led in some way by Mrs. Ida Davison herself. As if she wanted her story to finally be told.

I hope that my writing this work does not offend any of the families directly involved in the events. Also, any facts which are misconstrued are accidental. I attempted to tell the story as unbiased as possible, and if there are any errors found within this work, it is due to my misunderstanding of the official records, and not due to me trying to manipulate the facts.

I encourage anyone who has enjoyed reading this work to visit The Davison Home someday. All proceeds from the tour donations go towards the upkeep of the home itself.

THE END

Complete Murder File

At 9:42 AM on Sept. 19, 1970 the dispatcher received a call for an ambulance and Police to come to 109 3rd Ave. North in reference to a lady being badly injured.

Upon arrival, officers entered through the rear door and found an elderly white female lying on the kitchen floor bleeding from the head and vaginal area and in an unconscious condition.

Victim was identified as Ida C. Davison 75 years of age and she was taken to the Galveston County Memorial Hospital where she died at 12 noon Sept. 19, 1970 without regaining consciousness.

Upon investigation it was learned that a young colored male was seen within the vicinity of the neighborhood.

Upon further investigation the suspect was identified a Johnie Avie colored male, 18 years of age.

Suspect was arrested at 5"17PM September 19, 1970 and charged with Murder With Malice.

TABLE OF CONTENTS

Table of Contents
Page 2

A-4 Hairnet Brown

A-5 Pubic Hair

A-6 Hair From Head

A-7 Blood Sample

A-8 Vaginal Smear

A-9 Finger Nail Clippings

A-10 Blood Scrappings From Right Hand

A-11 Photos at Gavleston Co. Mem. Hosp.

A-12 Photos at County Morgue

A-13 Finger Prints

EXHIBIT B Suspect Johnie Avie

B-1 Shirt, Brown Nylon

B-2 Pants, Gold Cut Off

B-3 Undershorts, Cotton Boxer Type

B-4 Sandel, Right Brown Leather

B-5 Left Sandel, Brown Leather

B-6 Pubic Hair

B-7 Hair From Head

B-8 Money From Property $3.00

EXHIBIT 'C'

C-1 Sheet, White From Hospital

237

Table of Contents
Page 3

238

No. 102

Police Department

COMPLAINT NO. 11386   DATE 9-19-70   TIME 0712

NAME   Manager Fishmarket   PHONE

ADDRESS   202 3rd. St. N.

REPORTS Sup. Boy.

                               DISP. Reno

OFFICER ASSIGNED   752-Cole

OFFICER REPORT   P O L

DATE 9-19-70   OFFICER W. Cole

No. 102

13389

Police Department

COMPLAINT NO. 11387   DATE 9-18970   TIME 0755

NAME   Mrs Rays   PHONE

ADDRESS   I^C fish market

REPORTS   Would like to see Officer

DISP Schoolcraft

OFFICER ASSIGNED   753 "ilmore

OFFICER REPORT   _see report_

DATE 9-19-70   OFFICER _Gilmor_

3 88

Police Department

COMPLAINT NO. 11388   DATE 9-19-70   TIME 0942

NAME (Rev.) didn't understand last name   PHONE

ADDRESS 3rd Ave & 1st N

REPORTS Women hurt badly need a amb.

Crowder notified

DISP. Schoolcraft

OFFICER ASSIGNED 737 Henry 739 Oliver

OFFICER REPORT

DATE 9-19-70   OFFICER

Form 105

OFFENSE REPORT
TEXAS CITY POLICE DEPARTMENT

OFFENSE Murder with Malice

COMPLAINANT Mrs. E. J. Opersteny   ADDRESS 416-10th Ave. North, Texas City

Bus. Phone _____ Res. Phone _____ Age _____ Sex Female Color White

Reported by Rev. Jesse Ruefenacht Address 102-2nd Ave. N. Texas City Phone 948-2784

Place of Occurrence 109-3rd Ave. N. Texas City, Texas

Date of Occurrence September 19, 1970   Time 7:45AM - 9:42 A.M./P.M.

Received by Dispatcher Date 9/19/70 Time 9:42 A.M./P.M. How Telephone

DETAILS OF OFFENSE

At the above time I received a call from the Dispatcher to go to 109-3rd
Ave. N. in reference to a call for the Police and an ambulance. Upon arrival,
I was directed to the rear of the house where I talked with Mr. & Mrs. Opersteny,
416 10th Ave. North. Mrs. Opersteny stated that at approximately 0900 hours,
date, she had attempted to telephone her mother, Mrs. Ida C. Davison, 75 DOB:
9-30-94, who resides at 109 3rd Ave. N. She said she got no answer, nor could she
get an answer after several attempts. She said that at approximately 0930 hours
she decided to go to her mothers to check on her as she knew she would be alone
as Mr. Davison usually leaves for work shortly prior to 0800 hours. She said
that when she and her husband arrived they looked through through the screen
door and saw her mother lying on the kitchen floor in blood. She said she then
started calling for someone to call the Police and an Ambulance.

I then talked with Rev. & Mrs. Ruefenacht and Rev. George Hawkins, P. O.
Box 1203, Rockport, who is staying with the Ruefenachts. They all stated, in

Preliminary Investigation by _____ W. R. Henry

Cleared by _____

Date _____ Signed _____ Rank _____

242

Form 105

OFFENSE REPORT
TEXAS CITY POLICE DEPARTMENT

OFFENSE

COMPLAINANT_____ADDRESS_____

Bus. Phone_____Res. Phone_____Age_____Sex_____Color_____

Reported by_____Address_____Phone_____

Place of Occurrence_____

Date of Occurrence_____Time_____ A. M.
                                                                     P. M.

Received by_____Date_____Time_____ A. M.
                                                          P. M. How_____

DETAILS OF OFFENSE

substance, that they heard Mr. Opersteny screaming and that Rev. Ruefenacht
called the Station.

Officer Oliver and I entered the Davison home through the kitchen door,
which is located on the southwest corner of the house. The screen door was
unlatched and the inner wooden door was standing open. Upon entering the kitchen
I observed the body of an elderly white female lying on the floor with the head
toward the back door. She was clad in a white slip under a pink and white housecoat, both of which were pushed above the waist exposing the lower half of the
body which was nude. The body was resting on it's back with the arms at the
sides, the legs were spread. There was a wound on the right forehead and the
head was sourrounded by a large amount of blood, both on the floor and on the
wall next to the head. There was also blood visible at the vaginal area indicating
that Mrs. Davison had been the victim of a criminal assault. Mrs. Davison was
unconscious, however, breathing could be detected. Chief DeWalt was notified
and arrived with Lt. Saragoza who conducted the crime scene investigation to
include photographs and dusting for fingerprints.

Preliminary Investigation by_____

Cleared by_____

Date_____Signed_____Rank_____

5

243

Form 105

File No.

OFFENSE REPORT
TEXAS CITY POLICE DEPARTMENT

OFFENSE

COMPLAINANT   ADDRESS

Bus. Phone   Res. Phone   Age   Sex   Color

Reported by   Address   Phone

Place of Occurrence

Date of Occurrence   Time   A. M.
                                                                        P. M.

Received by   Date   Time   A. M.
                                                     P. M. How

DETAILS OF OFFENSE

    Mrs. Davison was transported to Galveston County Memorial Hospital

be Crowder Ambulance Svc. where she was attended by Dr's D. H. Eames

and C. Born. Mrs. Davison expired at 1200 hours and the Deputy Medical

Investigator ordered the body transferred to John Sealy Hospital, Galveston,

for investigation by the Medical Examiner. Dr. Kurt Weiss, Deputy Medical

Examiner, Galveston County, was contacted by Chief DeWalt and appraised of

the information gathered by this Department relative to Mrs. Davison.

    Investigation of the scene indicated that the victim was possible sitting at

the kitchen table when attacked. A newspaper which was on the table, at the

corner had blood on it which indicated the victim had fallen face down on it.

A woman's black purse was on the table but did not appear to have been disturbed.

There was a coffee cup on the table which showed traces of what appeared to be

coffee. A toaster, located next to the stove, which is south of the table, had

two pieces of toasted bread in the raised position which were still soft.   There

Preliminary Investigation by

Cleared by

Date   Signed   Rank

6.

Form 105

OFFENSE REPORT
TEXAS CITY POLICE DEPARTMENT

OFFENSE

COMPLAINANT ADDRESS

Bus. Phone Res. Phone Age Sex Color

Reported by Address Phone

Place of Occurrence

Date of Occurrence Time A. M. P. M.

Received by Date Time P. M. How A. M.

DETAILS OF OFFENSE

was a large amount of water on the floor which appeared to have come from an overflowing sink. One side of the sink was filled to the top and one other side was filled approximately halfway with water. On the floor near the sink, in the water, lay a pair of female white underpants. It was noted that the crotch of the underpants had been ripped. A human tooth was found near the table and another was found in the blood under the head of the victim and one on the floor next to the victims head. There was no indication of a struggle in the kitchen.

The remainder of the house was checked however no one was found nor were there indications that anything had been disturbed.

A neighborhood check was made by Officer's Oliver, Eden, Gilmore, and this officer. Some small children who reside in the house across the alley from Mrs. Davison advised Officer Oliver that earlier they had heard the Davison's dog barking however they did not see anyone around the house. Mr. Edward Swann, 204 1st Str. N. stated that shortly prior to 0800 he heard what he thought was a

Preliminary Investigation by

Cleared by

Date Signed Rank

7.

Form 105

File No.____

OFFENSE REPORT
TEXAS CITY POLICE DEPARTMENT

OFFENSE____

COMPLAINANT____ ADDRESS____

Bus. Phone____ Res. Phone____ Age____ Sex____ Color____

Reported by____ Address____ Phone____

Place of Occurrence____

Date of Occurrence____ Time____ A. M. P. M.

Received by____ Date____ Time____ A. M. P. M. How____

DETAILS OF OFFENSE

scream but thought it was either children or someone having a family argument.

Rev. Reufenacht stated that at approximately 0830 he was in the alley behind

the Davison home looking for his dog however he did not see or hear anything

unusual.

Preliminary Investigation by____

Cleared by____

Date____ Signed____ Rank____

8.

Form 195-A

File No. _____ **A47360**

SUPPLEMENTARY OFFENSE REPORT

TEXAS CITY POLICE DEPARTMENT

OFFENSE ___Murder With Malice_____ COMPLAINANT _Mrs. E. J. Opersteny___

LOCATION_109-3rd Ave. North Texas City_____ ADDRESS _____

DETAILS OF OFFENSE, PROGRESS OF INVESTIGATION, ETC.

DATE OF OFFENSE_____Sept. 19, 1970_____

While investigating the murder of Mrs. Ida C. Davison w/f 75 the following facts were learned.

Officer George Eden, while on routine patrol at about 7:45 AM observed Johnie Avie c/m 18 address #6 Bay Str. So. walking south in the 200 block of 3rd Str. North.

Officer Eden stated he received the call to the I-c Fish Market in reference to a suspecious person along with Officer Gilmore but was unable to locate Avie again.

Officer Gilmore stated that while enroute to the I-C Fish Market at about 7:55 AM he observed a tall c/m wearing brown undershirt and short gold colored pants walking in the 200 block of 3rd Ave. North.

Officer Gilmore stated that Mrs. Carmen Reyer, owner and operator of the Fish Market described the suspicious person that she reported as being dressed the same way as the subject observed by Officer Gilmore.

Local units advised of information received.

Information pending.

CLEARED BY_____

DATE_____ SIGNED___Oliver_____
(Investigating Officer)

7.

Form 105-A

File No. **A47360**

SUPPLEMENTARY OFFENSE REPORT

TEXAS CITY POLICE DEPARTMENT

OFFENSE _____ Murder With Malice _____ COMPLAINANT _____ Mrs. E. J. Operateny _____

LOCATION _____ 109 3rd Ave. North, Texas City _____ ADDRESS _____

DETAILS OF OFFENSE, PROGRESS OF INVESTIGATION, ETC.

DATE OF OFFENSE _____ Sept. 19, 1970 _____

Received a call along with Officer Henry to 109 3rd Ave. N. in reference to an injured person. Upon arrival officers interviewed persons present and learned that foul play was indicated.

Officers Henry and I entered the house and found Mrs. Ida C. Davison w/f 75 lying on the kitchen floor and bleeding from the head and bleeding from the vaginal area. Mrs. Davison had lacerations on the head and was bleeding from the mouth. For further details see officer Henry's report attached.

Information on the scene revealed that both rear and front doors were unlocked. Both screens were closed but unlocked and both wooden doors were open. A search was then conducted of all rooms on all levels with negative results.

Upon arrival of Chief DeWalt I then departed the scene and Proceeded to Galveston Co. Memorial Hosp. where Mrs. Davison was taken by Crowder Ambulance. Upon arrival I talked to Dr. C. Born, Neuro-Surgeon and Dr. Eames M. D. who reported Mrs. Davison was in critical condition with a fractured skull and possible brain damage.

Dr. Eames reported severe damage to the vaginal area but was unable

CLEARED BY _____

DATE _____ SIGNED _____

(Investigating Officer)

10.

File No. _____ **A47360**

ᴜᴘPLEMENTARY OFFENSE REᴘ ᴏ ᴛ

TEXAS CITY POLICE DEPARTMENT

OFFENSE ___ MURDER WITH MALICE _____ COMPLAINANT __ Mrs. Opcrateny _____

LOCATION __ 109 3rd Ave, North Texas City ____ ADDRESS _____

DETAILS OF OFFENSE, PROGRESS OF INVESTIGATION, ETC.

DATE OF OFFENSE _____ Sept 19, 1970 ____

to determine to what extent.

While in the examination room Dr. Born removed clothing from Mrs. Davison as requested and gave them to me wrapped in a white sheet. Clothing consisted of one white gown, one red/white stripe cotton house coat. The items were cut off with scissors. Hair net was also removed.

Mrs. Davison was taken to the X-Ray room where she was in constant care of Dr. Born and Eames. At 12 noon 9/19/70 Mrs. Davison expired and was pronounced dead by Dr. Born in the X-Ray room.

At this time I scraped dried blood from the right hand of Mrs. Davison and placed the traces in an envelope furnished by the hospital. The nails were also scraped and clipped into a separate envelope which was tagged as evidence.

Sgt. Joe Standley, Galbeston Co. deputy Med. examiner arrived and consucted necessary investigation and then ordered the body removed to the Med. Examating Officer at John Sealey for autopsy. The body was removed by Emkin-Linton Funeral Service.

1445 hrs 9/19/70

I proceeded to John Sealey Morgue where I was met by deputy Cornor

CLEARED BY _____

DATE _____ SIGNED _____

(Investigating Officer)

//

Form 105-A

File No. _____ **A47360**

SUPPLEMENTARY OFFENSE REPORT

TEXAS CITY POLICE DEPARTMENT

OFFENSE __Murder With Malice_____ COMPLAINANT __Mrs. E. J. Operafrny____

LOCATION __109 3rd Ave. North, Texas City_____ ADDRESS _____

DETAILS OF OFFENSE, PROGRESS OF INVESTIGATION, ETC.

DATE OF OFFENSE ___Sept. 19, 1970_____

Dr. Kurt Weiss, who performed the Autopsy.

Dr. Weiss reported the Cause of Death was due to a fractured skull and extensive brain damage which was the result of a severe blow with a blunt instryment.

Dr. Weiss reported the instrument could have been a fist.

Dr. Weiss also stated that Mrs. Davison had damage to the vaginal area caused by penetration. Damage was found to be 5 to 6 inches deep and could have been caused by a penis. Dr. Weiss stated he would consult with Dr. Buckley on Monday for final results.

Dr. Weiss gave me pubic hair and also hair from Mrs. Davison's head which was marked as such. Also received was a vaginal smear and a vile of blood. All items were brought to the station and tagged as evidence.

1717 Hrs 9-19-70

Officers Fred Monroe and Goerge Eden came to the station with Johnie Avie c/m 18 Address #6 Bay Str So. charged with old traffic and investigation Subject was booked and confined to jail. When subject was placed in cell his clothing was removed which consisted of one brown slip over undershirt, one gold colored pair of cut off pants, one pair of cotton shorts and a pair of leather sandels. These items were taken to the ID Department where they were inspected.

CLEARED BY_____

DATE_____ SIGNED_____

(Investigating Officer)

/2.

Form 105-A

File No. _____ **A47360**

SUPPLEMENTARY OFFENSE REPORT

TEXAS CITY POLICE DEPARTMENT

OFFENSE ____ Murder With Malice _____ COMPLAINANT ___ Mrs. E. J. Operatony ___

LOCATION ____ 109 3rd Ave. North _____ ADDRESS _____

DETAILS OF OFFENSE, PROGRESS OF INVESTIGATION, ETC.

DATE OF OFFENSE ___ Sept. 19, 1970 _____

Inspection revealed a large amount of blood in the front of the shorts and pants. Also blood spots were found on the shirt.

6:30 PM 9-19-70

Judge Ted Bishop arrived at the station as requested at which time Johnie Avie was given his Statutory Warning and advised of his Right by Judge Bishop.

6:35PM 9-19-70

Subject was again advised of his rights and signed a waiver of rights form stating he did understand.

Subject was then interviewed and denied any knowledge of the murder.

Subject later admitted entering the Davison home at approximately 0800 hrs. 9-19-70 and stated he went to the home to steal money and found Mrs. Davison lying in the kitchen floor.

2040 Hrs 9-19-70

Subject gave a voluntary statement to this effect.

2117 hrs. 9-19-70

Subject gave a second voluntary statement admitting that he entered the victims home and admitted that he raped Mrs. Davison but denied striking her or taking any merchandise.

CLEARED BY_____

DATE_____ SIGNED_____
(Investigating Officer)

23.

SUPPLEMENTARY OFFENSE REPORT

TEXAS CITY POLICE DEPARTMENT

OFFENSE___ Murder with Malice _____COMPLAINANT___ Mrs. E. J. Opersteny

LOCATION___109 3rd Ave. N. _____ ADDRESS _____

DETAILS OF OFFENSE, PROGRESS OF INVESTIGATION, ETC.

DATE OF OFFENSE___Sept. 19, 1970

10:10 9-19-70

Judge Ted Bishop arrived and accepted a formal complaint on Johnie Avie charged in Murder W/Malice. Warrant issued.

10:15 PM 9-19-70

Judge Bishop again advised Avie of his rights and also of the formal complaint.

Subject stated to Judge that he did understand.

Subject confined to jail.

12:05PM 9-20-70

Subject was again advised of his rights after which he admitted entering the house for the purpose of stealing some money. Subject stated he found the victim lying on the floor and proceded to rape her. The victim tried to push him off at which time the subject struck her with his fist in the face. Subject then went upstairs to a bed room and stole some money. Subject stated he then went to the home of Johnie McDaniel Address 109 1st Ave. North and slept until about 11AM and then went to town and got into a dice game with a Bruce Montgomery.

Subject gave a voluntary statement to this effect.

CLEARED BY_____

DATE_____ SIGNED_____

(Investigating Officer)

14

Form 105-A

File No. _____ A47360

ꙄUPPLEMENTARY OFFENSE REꝏRT

TEXAS CITY POLICE DEPARTMENT

OFFENSE _____ Murder with Malice _____ COMPLAINANT _____ Mrs. E. J. Operateny

LOCATION _____ 109 3rd Ave. N. _____ ADDRESS _____

DETAILS OF OFFENSE, PROGRESS OF INVESTIGATION, ETC.

DATE OF OFFENSE _____ Sept. 19, 1970

12:10PM 9-20-70

Mrs. Carmen Reyes M/F Address 319 3rd Ave. No. came to the station
as requested and gave a voluntary affidavit stating she saw Avie at the I-C Fish
Market several times between 0650 9-19-70 and 0800 9-19-70.

Mrs. Reyes stated the subject looked and acted very strange and described
the clothing as those the subject was wearing when arrested. Officer Henry took
the affidavit.

1:58PM 9-20-70

Mrs. Sarah Parker c/f Address 216 3rd Avenue North came to the station
as requested and gave a voluntary statement stating she saw Johnie Avie
several times between 1650 and 8Am 9-19-70 and stated the subject looked and
acted very strange. Mrs. Parker stated she talked to Avie and believes he was
drunk or drugged.

Mrs. Parker gave Officer Henry a Vol affidavit.

Further investigation pending.

12:45PM 9-20-70

Avie voluntarily gave a sample of pubic hair and also hair pulled from his

CLEARED BY _____

DATE _____ SIGNED _____

(Investigating Officer)

15.

253

SUPPLEMENTARY OFFENSE REPORT

File No. _____ A47360

TEXAS CITY POLICE DEPARTMENT

OFFENSE ___ Murder With Malice _____ COMPLAINANT ___ Mrs. E. J. Operstany ___

LOCATION ___ 109 3rd Ave. North _____ ADDRESS _____

DETAILS OF OFFENSE, PROGRESS OF INVESTIGATION, ETC.

DATE OF OFFENSE ___ Sept. 19, 1970 ___

head. The subject pulled the hair himself which was tagged as evidence.

11AM 9-21-70

Lt. Saragoza and Officer Oliver went to DPS Laboratory in Houston and upon arrival we contected DPS Chemist Dennis Ramsey who took custody of property exhibits A-1 thru A-10 which is property removed from the victim. Exhibit B-1 thru B-7 removed from suspect and exhibits C-1 Hospital sheet and exhibits D-1 thru D-5 evidence found at the scene.

Mr. Ramsey took custody at 12:17PM 9-21-70 with a request for comparison and analysis of above to determine suspect Johnie Avie c/m 18 involvement in this crime.

1500 hrs. 9-21-70

Johnie Avie c/m 18 was cleared through the booking office for transfer to Galveston County jail. Subject was taken directly from the station to the office of Dr. G. F. Quinn office address 511 9th Ave. N. where the subject was examined by the Doctor.

Subject was then transferred by Officer Eden and myself to Galveston County jail where he was released to booking officer at 1544 hrs. 9-21-70.

CLEARED BY _____

DATE _____ SIGNED ___ David Oliver _____
(Investigating Officer)

16.

LAST NAME	FIRST NAME	INITIAL	ALIASES (If several, write them at bottom)				ARREST NO
AVIE	JOHNNY		DOB	8-20-52			51319

RESIDENCE		Prct.	Sex	Color	Age	OCCUPATION
#6- BAY ST.			M F X	W N M O	18	CONST.

Date Time of Arrest	Place Arrested	Prct.	Arresting Officer	Badge No
9-19-70	6th.ST. & 2nd.AVE.S.		MONROE	500
1717				

Charge When Booked.

OLD TRAFFIC AND ~~████~~ MURDER   Charge Changed to   9-19-70

FORMAL CHARGE OF MURDER W/MALICE FILED WITH JUDGE BISHOP 2210 HRS

FACTS OF ARREST (Describe specific act for which prisoner was arrested)

SUBJ ADVISED OF RIGHTS BY JUDGE BISHOP AT 1830 HRS 9-19-70

SUBJ ADVISED OF RIGHTS BY JUDGE BISHOP AT 2215 HRS 9-19-70

Visited Father 9-20-70 at 9:45 AM

1845 HR 9-19-70 Sub, Ref To use Phone & Requested DORATY No Visitors DTO

1500 HRS 9 21-70 TRANSfered To Co Jail he

Arrest Record   Texas City, Texas Police Dept.   Ident. No.

Oliver & Eden

Arrest No.

POLICE DEPARTMENT
Texas-City, Texas

Date: 9-19-70

Name: Johnny Avie   Offense

Cash 4 50   Personal Property, to wit: _____

_____ 50¢ (166) _____

_____ 1¢ _____ cards _____

Property Confiscated by Police 9-20-70

Booking Office: _____   Arresting Officer: Monroe

Remarks: _____

Received property enumerated.   Date: 9-21-70

_____ Witness   _____ Prisoner's Signature

255

ATUTORY WARNIN
TEXAS C.C.P. ART. 15.17 (REVISED)

On this the 19th day of SEPTEMBER , 19 70 , personally

appeared JOHNNY AVIE , age 18 , who had

been arrested by OFFICERS EDEN & MONROE , a peace officer at TEXAS

CITY , Galveston County, Texas at 5:17 A.M. /P. M., on

19 SEPTEMBER , 19 70 , and who was in the custody of _Officer Savage_

Stanley + Olins, a peace officer of TEXAS CITY POLICE DEPARTMENT ,

Galveston County, Texas, and I gave the said JOHNNY AVIE

the following warning:

JOHNNY AVIE
Name

(1) You have been accused of the offense of _Murder_ .

(2) You have a right to retain counsel.

(3) You have a right to remain silent.

(4) You have a right to have an attorney present during any interview
with peace officers or attorneys representing the State.

(5) You have the right to terminate the interview at any time.

(6) You have the right to request the appointment of counsel, if you are
indigent and cannot afford counsel.

(7) You have the right to an examining trial.

(8) You are not required to make a statement and that any statement
made by you may be used against you.

*Your bail is set at _____ **

(OR)

*Bail is denied. If a formal complaint is filed against you, your bail
will then be set. ***

WAIVER-OF-RIGHTS FORM

On the _19ᵗʰ_ day of _September_ , 19 _70_

Dail Oline _____ advised
            (Officer)

Johnny Avie _____ that he did not have to
         (Subject)

tell him anything; that anything he did tell him might be used in evidence

against him in a court of law; that he had a right to an attorney; that he had

a right to have the attorney present while the officer was talking to him or

questioning him; that he did not have to say anything to the officer until his

attorney or lawyer was present; that if he talked to the officers he could ter-

minate or stop talking to the officers any time he wanted to and that any time

he desired, an attorney would be called to assist him and no questions would

be asked him until the attorney arrived.

Johnny Avie _____
               (Signature of subject)

I, _Dail Oline_ _____ , a member of the

Tyus City Police Dept _____ on the _19_ day of

September , 19 _70_ , administered the foregoing warning to

Johnny Avie _____ before commencing an inter-
      (Subject)

view with him.

Dail Oline _____
              (Signature of officer)

(If the subject refuses to sign this waiver, the officer should so note)

20   1835   9-19-70

257

TEXAS CITY POLICE DEPARTMENT

VOLUNTARY STATEMENT OF JOHNNY AVIE

19 SEPTEMBER , A.D., 19 70

I, JOHNNY AVIE , before being interrogated and after

first being duly warned by JUDGE TED BISHOP of TEXAS CITY, GALVESTON
(name of magistrate)   (county or city)

at 6:30 P. M., at TEXAS CITY POLICE DEPARTMENT on 19 SEPTEMBER 1970
(time)   (location)   (date)

of the accusation against me of MURDER and the affidavit,
(charge or offense)

if any, filed in support of such accusation; that I have a right to retain counsel; that I have a right to remain silent; that I have a right to have an attorney present during any interview with peace officers or attorneys representing the State; that I have the right to terminate the interview at any time; that if I am unable to afford and obtain counsel, I have the right to request the appointment of counsel; that I have the right to have an examining trial; that I am not required to make any statement at all, and that any statement I do make may be used against me; and DERIL OLIVER , the person to whom this
(officer taking statement)

statement is made, also warned me at the beginning of the interrogation that I have the right to have a lawyer present to advise me either prior to any questioning or during any questioning; that if I am unable to employ a lawyer, I have the right to have a lawyer appointed to counsel with me prior to or during any questioning; that I have the right to remain silent; that I do not have to make any statement at all and that any statement made by me may be used in evidence against me at my trial, do hereby make the following voluntary statement:

My name is JOHNNY AVIE . I live at #10 E Olender Homes GALVESTON, GALVESTON TEXAS WITH MY MOTHER AND FATHER. I AM 18 YEARS OLD AND WORK ON CONSTRUCTION.

AT ABOUT 8:00 AM THIS MORNING, SATURDAY THE 19TH DAY OF SEPTEMBER 1970 I WENT TO THE OLD GREEN CASTLE ON THIRD AVENUE NORTH. I WENT THERE FOR THE PURPOSE OF STEALING SOME MONEY FROM THE PEOPLE THAT LIVE THERE. I KNOW THE PEOPLE BUT CAN NOT REMEMBER THEIR NAME. I FIRST WENT AROUND THE HOUSE AND LOOKED THROUGH THE WINDOWS BUT DID NOT SEE ANYONE. I NOTICED THE FRONT DOOR WAS OPEN SO I WENT INSIDE AND WENT TO THE KITCHEN. I FIRST NOTICED THE LADY THAT LIVES THERE WAS LYING IN THE KITCHEN FLOOR AND WAS BLEEDING FROM THE MOUTH. THERE WAS A LOT OF BLOOD ON THE FLOOR UNDER HER.

I FIRST WENT TO THE REFRIGERATOR AND OPENED IT UP AND LOOKED INSIDE AND THEN WENT UP STAIRS TO ONE OF THE BED ROOMS AND LOOKED AROUND FOR SOME MONEY. AFTER AWHILE I GOT SCARED AND STARTED RUNNING. I RAN OUT THE FRONT DOOR AND WENT TO MR JOHNNY McDANIELD HOUSE ON FIRST AVE NORTH.

THE CLOTHING AND SHOES THAT I WAS WEARING WHEN THE POLICE PICKED ME UP IS THE SAME CLOTHING I WAS WEARING WHEN I WENT INTO THE GREEN CASTLE ON THIRD AVENUE NORTH.

TEXAS CITY POLICE DEPARTMENT

VOLUNTARY STATEMENT OF ___JOHNNY AVIE___

19 SEPTEMBER _____, A.D., 19 70

I, ___JOHNNY AVIE_____, before being interrogated and after

first being duly warned by___JUDGE TED BISHOP_____ of____TEXAS CITY, GALVESTON_
                              (name of magistrate)   (county or city)

at __6:30__ P. M., at _TEXAS CITY POLICE DEPARTMENT_____ on __19 SEPTEMBER 1970___
   (time)   (location)   (date)

of the accusation against me of_____MURDER_____ and the affidavit,
                                   (charge or offense)

if any, filed in support of such accusation; that I have a right to retain counsel; that I have a right to remain
silent; that I have a right to have an attorney present during any interview with peace officers or attorneys
representing the State; that I have the right to terminate the interview at any time; that if I am unable to
afford and obtain counsel, I have the right to request the appointment of counsel; that I have the right to
have an examining trial; that I am not required to make any statement at all, and that any statement I do

make may be used against me; and _DERIL OLIVER_____, the person to whom this
                                      (officer taking statement)

statement is made, also warned me at the beginning of the interrogation that I have the right to have a lawyer
present to advise me either prior to any questioning or during any questioning; that if I am unable to employ
a lawyer, I have the right to have a lawyer appointed to counsel with me prior to or during any questioning;
that I have the right to remain silent; that I do not have to make any statement at all and that any statement
made by me may be used in evidence against me at my trial, do hereby make the following voluntary statement:

My name is ___JOHNNY AVIE_____ I live at ___#10 E. OLEANDER OLEANDER HOMES GALVESTON,

TEXAS WITH MY MOTHER AND FATHER. I AM 18 YEARS OLD AND WORK ON CONSTRUCTION.

AT ABOUT 8:00 AM THIS MORNING, SATURDAY SEPTEMBER 19, 1970 I WENT TO THE OLD GREEN

CASTLE ON THIRD AVENUE NORTH. I WENT THERE FOR THE PURPOSE OF STEALING SOME MONEY FROM THE

PEOPLE THAT LIVE THERE. I KNOW THE PEOPLE BUT CAN NOT REMEMBER THEIR NAME. I FIRST WENT

AROUND THE HOUSE AND LOOKED THROUGH ALL THE WINDOWS BUT DID NOT SEE ANYONE. I NOTICED THE FRONT

DOOR WAS OPEN SO I WENT INSIDE AND WENT TO THE KITCHEN. I SAW THE LADY THAT LIVES THERE

LYING ON THE KITCHEN FLOOR WITH BLOOD ON HER. I SAW THAT SHE WAS HELPLESS SO I RAPED HER.

I ONLY RAPED HER ONCE AND WHEN I FINISHED I WENT TO THE REFRIGERATOR AND OPENED IT UP.

I THEN WENT UP STAIRS TO ONE OF THE BEDROOMS AND LOOKED FOR SOME MONEY.

WHILE I WAS IN THE BEDROOM I GOT SCARED AND STARTED RUNNING. I RAN OUT THE FRONT DOOR

WHICH WAS THE SAME ON I HAD ENTERED. I WENT TO JOHNNY McDANIELS HOUSE ON FIRST AVENUE NORTH

AND WENT TO SLEEP UNTIL AROUND 11:00 AM.

THE CLOTHING I WAS WEARING WHEN THE POLICE PICKED ME UP WAS THE SAME CLOTHING THAT I

WAS WEARING WHEN I WENT INTO THE GREEN CASTLE THIS MORNING.

259

No. 21,060

COMPLAINT

THE STATE OF TEXAS

vs.

Johnny Avie

Filed 19th day of Sept., 1970

Justice of the Peace, Precinct No. 5,

Galveston County, Texas.

WITNESSES:

D-136—COMPLAINT—Affidavit for Warrant of Arrest—(Short Form)—Class 1. (Arts. 507 and 509, C C P)

In the Name and by Authority of the State of Texas:

BEFORE ME, the undersigned authority, on this day personally appeared _D. Aleril_

Alvin, T.C.P.D.

who, after being by me duly sworn, on oath deposes and says That heretofore, to-wit, on or about the _19th_

day of _Sept_ A.D. 19 _70_, and before the making and filing of this Complaint, in

the County of _Galveston_ and State of Texas,

JOHNNY AKIE

did then and there unlawfully* _Murder with malice_

against the peace and dignity of the State.

David Aleril
Complainant

Sworn to and subscribed before me, this _19th_ day of _Sept_ A.D. 19 _70_

David Alvin

S. Johnson Justice of the Peace,

Precinct No. _____ _Galveston_ County, Texas.

*Here describe specifically the offense committed.

261

D-841

File No. 21000

IN JUSTICE'S COURT, Precinct No. 5

of Galveston County.

THE STATE OF TEXAS
VS.

Johnny Davis

WARRANT OF ARREST

Issued 19 day of Sept, 1920

_____ J. P.

Precinct No. 5, Gale Co., Texas.

D-844—WARRANT OF ARREST OR CAPIAS—Class 1. (C. C. P., Arts. 2501-2502) Cocke & Cowan, Inc.

THE STATE OF TEXAS

To any Peace Officer of the State of Texas, Greeting:

YOU ARE HEREBY COMMANDED to arrest _____ JOHNNY AVIE _____

_____ if to be found in your County, and bring _____ him _____ before me, a justice of the Peace in and for Precinct No. 5

of _____ _____ County, Texas, at my office in _____ Terlingua _____

in said County, on the _____ day of _____, 19 _____, at _____ o'clock _____ M., then and there

to answer the STATE OF TEXAS for an offense against the laws of said State, to-wit: _____ Murder _____

_____ with Malice _____

of _____ several felons _____ of which offense _____ he _____ is _____ accused by the written complaint, under oath,

_____ _____ _____ filed before me.

Herein Fail Not, but of this writ make due return showing how you have executed the same.

Witness my official signature, this _____ 14th _____ day of _____, 19 _____ 70 _____

Precinct No. _____ _____ _____, Justice of the Peace,

_____ County, Texas.

THE STATE OF TEXAS
COUNTY OF GALVESTON

Before me, the undersigned authority in and for said county and state, on this the ___20th___

day of ___September___ A. D. 19 70 , personally appeared __Mrs. Carmen Rivera Reyes__ ,
who after being by me duly sworn, deposes and says:

My name is Carmen Rivera Reyes. I am 44 years old and reside at 319 3rd Avenue

North, Texas City, Texas. I am the owner and operator of the IC Fish Market &

Grocery, which is located at 202 3rd Street N., Texas City.

At approximately 6:55 A.M., yesterday, September 19, I left my house to walk

to the Store. I walked east on 3rd Ave N., and turned south on 3rd St N. As I

turned the corner I saw a colored male in approximately the middle of the block,

bending over slapping at his legs. As I got close to him he looked up and I

recognized him as one of the Avie boys. He was wearing a pair of goldish brown

cut-off pants, a goldish brown undershirt and a pair of sandels. As I passed him

I spoke to him and asked him if the mosquitoes were biting him. He said "yes"

and I went on to the store. After I opened the store a customer, Mrs. Sarah

Parker, who lives on 3rd St N., came in, bought some coffee, and told me to be

careful because she said that after I went into the store the boy I had spoken

to had come over to the store and peeked in the window and then run back across

the street. After I let Mrs. Parker out I locked the door and would only open

it to let customers in. Several times I saw the Avie boy come up to the door

and try to open it and then leave. After he had come to the door several times

I looked at him and noticed that his eyes looked strange and thought he was

either drunk or doped up. I then called the Police and asked them to keep a

check on my store. The boy came back to the store several more times and tried

the door and at about 8:00 A.M. I decided to call the Police again. I did'nt

see the boy anymore after calling the Police.

Mrs Carmen Rivera Reyes

Subscribed and sworn to before me, the undersigned authority, on this the ___20th___ day of

___September___ 19 70 _J. D. Schraeder_

WITNESS: _I C Reyes_ Notary Public in and for Galveston County, Texas

WITNESS: _William R Terry_

My Commission Expires

6-1-71

27. 12:10 PM 9-20-70

264

THE STATE OF TEXAS
COUNTY OF GALVESTON

Before me, the undersigned authority in and for said county and state, on this the ____ 20th ____

day of ___ September ____ A. D. 19 70 , personally appeared __ Mrs. Sarah Parker ____ ,
who after being by me duly sworn, deposes and says:

My name is Sarah Henson Parker. I am 57 years old and reside at 216 3rd Ave N.,
Texas City, Texas. I am employed as a Maid at Leon's Motel, 626 2nd Ave N., in
Texas City.

At approximately 6:30 A.M., yesterday, September 19, I was looking out the window

of my house watching for Mrs. Reyes, at the IC Fish Market to open the store as I

was out of coffee. As I was watching I saw a young colored male run across the

street in the middle of the block of the 200 Block of 3rd St N. He came from the

east side of the street and I saw him run into the alley on the west side of the

street. A few minutes later I saw Mrs. Reyes walking toward her store on 3rd St

in the 200 Block. I then left my house and started walking to the store. As I

turned the corner onto 3rd St I saw the same boy run back across the street and

saw him peeking in the window of the store. As I got close to him I recognized

him as Johnny Avis, who I call "Pie." Her was wearing a pair of goldish brown

cut-off pants, and a goldish brown undershirt. I asked him what he had on his

mind and told him that whatever it was it wasn't right. He said he didn't have

nuthing on his mind and I told him then he better go home. He said O.K. and I

saw him go behind the house located next to the store. I noticed when I was talking

to him that he acted strange and he had a funny look in his eyes. I then went

into the store and got my coffee. When I left the store I started walking north

on 3rd St. When I got past the house next to the Store I turned around and saw

"Pie" in front of the store looking in the window again. I then went back to the

store and told Mrs. Reyes to lock her doors and to call the Police. I then went

home. Approximately 20 minutes later I left my house to go to work. As I came

out the door I saw "Pie" walking east on 3rd Ave N. in front of my house. It

Sarah Henson Parker

Subscribed and sworn to before me, the undersigned authority, on this the ___ 20 th ___ day of

September 19 70   *J. D. Schroeder*
WITNESS: *(signature)*   (Notary Public in and for Galveston County, Texas

WITNESS:

would have been about 20 minutes to 8 when I left the house. I talked to "Pie"

again and asked him why he had dropped out of school and told he ought to go back.

He said "O.K., Mama Sarah", and then continued walking east on 3rd Ave N. I then

went on to work.

Sarah Johnson Parker

THE STATE OF TEXAS
COUNTY OF GALVESTON

Before me, the undersigned authority in and for said county and state, on this the **24th** day of SEPTEMBER A. D. 19 70 personally appeared BRUCE NATHANIEL MONTGOMERY who after being by me duly sworn, deposes and says:

MY NAME IS BRUCE NATHANIEL MONTGOMERY, I AM 17 YEARS OLD AND LIVE AT 421-2nd AVENUE

SOUTH, TEXAS CITY, TEXAS.

AT ABOUT 1:00 PM ON SATURDAY THE 19th DAY OF SEPTEMBER 1970 I WAS WALKING WITH SOME

MORE GUYS PAST JOHNSONS POOL HALL WHEN JOHNNIE AVIE CAME OUT OF THE POOL HALL AND ASKED

US WHERE WE WERE GOING. I TOLD HIM WE WERE GOING TO THE OLD BOOKER T SCHOOL. JOHNNIE

STARTED WALKING WITH US AND WHEN WE GOT TO THE SCHOOL WE STARTED SHOOTING DICE. SOME

MORE GUYS CAME UP AND GOT INTO THE GAME BUT I DIDN'T PAY ANY ATTENTION XXXXX WHO THEY

WERE. WE PLAYED PLAYED FOR ABOUT AN HOUR AND THEN LEFT. JOHNNIE, MYSELF AND THE OTHER

THREE GUYS STARTED WALKING BACK TOWARD MY HOUSE WHEN I HEARD JOHNNIE SAY HE HAD BETTER

GO THE OTHER WAY BECAUSE THE LAW WAS LOOKING FOR HIM. HE DIDN'T SAY ANY BUT TOOK OFF IN

THE OPPOSITE DIRECTION FROM ME. I HAVN'T SEEN HIM SINCE.

JOHNNIE WAS WEARING A BROWN NYLON SHIRT,,BROWN SHORT PANTS AND SANDLES.

WE SEPERATED ABOUT 2:30 PM

Nathaniel Montgomery

Subscribed and sworn to before me, the undersigned authority, on this the 24th day of September 19 70 L. D. Schrader
Notary Public in and for Galveston County, Texas
My Commission Expires
6-1-71

70   1705   9 24 70

September 21, 1970
_____
(Date)

Laboratory
Texas Department of Public Safety

~~AUSTIN~~

Chief Rankin L. DeWalt, Department Of Police
of ~~Texas City,~~ ,Texas, submitted to___Department Of
~~Public Safety, Chemist~~ the following

Items Marked As Follows:

Exhibit A-1 Through A-10 removed from victim, Ida C. Davison W/F 75

Exhibit B-1 Through B-7 removed from suspect, Johnny Avie C/M 18

Exhibit C-1 Hospital Sheet Where Victim Lay

Exhibit D-1 Through D-5, evidence found at crime scene

It is requested that an examination be made to determine:

Comparison and analysis of above to determine suspect Johnnie (nmn) AVIE's

involvement in this crime.

Case Record Information:

Offense: Murder with Malice
Date of Offense: September 19, 1970
County of Offense: Galveston County, Texas

Suspect: Full name, color, sex, age   Johnnie (nmn) AVIE; Negro Male; age 18
                                        D.O.B. August 20, 1952
Victim: Full name, color, sex, age   IDA C. DAVISON; White Female; age 75

Please send copy of report to: Chief of Police, Rankin L. DeWalt; Department
~~of Police;~~ 920 - 5th Avenue North; Texas City, Texas 77590

_____
(Name)

_____
(Official Title)

42-3

Exhibit A-1 through A-10, removed from victim, Ida C. DAVISON

    A-1 House coat
    A-2 Slip
    A-3 Underpants
    A-4 Hairnet
    A-5 Pubic Hair
    A-6 Hair from head
    A-7 Blood sample
    A-8 Vaginal smear
    A-9 Finger nail clippings
    A-10 Blood scrapings from right hand

Exhibit "B#1 through B-7, removed from suspect, Johnnie (nmn) AVIE

    B-1 Shirt
    B-2 pants
    B-3 Shorts
    B-4 Sandel, right
    B-5 Sandel, left
    B-6 Pubic hair
    B-7 Hair from head

Exhibit C-1, from Galveston County Memorial Hospital

    C-1 bed sheet

Exhibit D-1 through D-5, evidence found at crime scene, 109 - 3rd Avenue North

    D-1 Hair from scene
    D-2 Hair from scene
    D-3 Teeth from victim (3)
    D-4 Grass on kitchen floor
    D-5 Sample of grass from yard

DEPARTMENT OF POLICE   t. No. __8 9 1 1__   F.   **A47360**

BUREAU OF CRIMINAL IDENTIFICATION   Classification _____

TEXAS CITY, TEXAS

Date and Time Examined __9/21/70 8:43 A.M.__   Color __Negro__   Sex __Male__ Battley SP No. _____

Date, Time and Place of Arrest __9/19/70 - 1717 - 6th St. & 2nd Ave. So.__   M.O. Field _____

Arrest No. __51319__   Case No. _____   F.B.I. No. _____   D.P.S. No. _____

Name __AVIE__   __Johnnie__   __(nnn)__   Married: __single__

        Last   First   Middle

Alias: __"Pie"__

Address __10-E Oleander Homes; Galveston, Texas__

Hair __B/K__   Eyes __Brn__   Height __6-4__   Weight __186__   Age __18__

Comp. __Drk__   Build __Tall__   Occ. __Construction Work__   Must. __none__

Date and Place of Birth __August 20, 1952 Ft. Hood, Texas__   Extraction: _____

Reg.: Citizen __U.S.A.__ Reg. U.S Mil Ser. __yes__ __No__ Place and Board No. __Galveston, Texas__   Mil. Class _____

Alien

Previous Military Service __none__   Serial Number _____

Last Place Employed __Morrison Construction Co. at Marathon in T. C.__   S. S. _____

Father __Jeffery Avie__   Address __10-E__

Mother __Louise Avie__   " __same__

Wife-Husband __none__

Sister __Bertha Lee Avie__   " __6th St. at Ted Perkins__

Brother __Zeffery Avie; Milton & Ricky__   " __10-E__

Son-Daughter __none__

F.P. and Photos Forward to: __P.O.   FBI   TCP   DPS__

Place of Parents Birth. Father __La.__   Mother __La.__

Arresting Officers __Eden-Monroe__   Division __TCP__

Charge or Crime __Murder: W/Malice__

Modus Operandi and Accomplices _____

Disposition _____

Prisoner's Signature __Johnnie Avie__

Processed By __Savas Saragoza__

New Photo and Description: Date _____ Age _____ Height _____ Weight _____   Right Thumb Print

                Date _____ Age _____ Height _____ Weight _____

                Date _____ Age _____ Height _____ Weight _____

Marks, Scars, sal sc center forehead; sc behind lt ear; 2½ sc inside rt

Tattoos, Teeth. none   round sc lt lower arm; 2½ sc inside rt leg above knee;

                        sc lt eyebrow near nose

Peculiarities: lt handed; 10th grade in school; admits arrest in T. C.

DEPARTMENT OF POLICE   No. 8 8 1 1   F

BUREAU OF CRIMINAL IDENTIFIC. .N   Classification   A47360

TEXAS CITY, TEXAS

Date and Time Examined 7/5/67 5:30 P.M.   Color Negro   Sex Male   Battley SP No.

Date, Time and Place of Arrest 7/5/67 1505 Menkes   M.O. Field

Arrest No. 44053   Case No.   F.B.I No.   D.P.S. No.

Name AVIE   Johnnie   (nmn)   Married Single
      Last   First   Middle

Alias "Pie"

Address 121 - 1st Ave. South

Hair B/K   Eyes D/Brn   Height 5-9½   Weight 135   Age 14

Comp. Drk   Build Sldr.   Occ. Unempl.grass cutter   Must None

Date and Place of Birth Aug. 20, 1952   Ft.Hood, Texas   Extraction

Reg.: Alien Citizen U.S.A. Yes   Reg. U.S Mil. Ser. No   Place and Board No. none   Mil. Class

Previous Military Service none   Serial Number

Last Place Employed Youth Corp, Pret #4   S. S.

Father Jeffery Avie   Address same
Mother Louise Avie   "   same
Wife-Husband none   "
Sister Bertha Avie   "   same
Brother Zeffery Avie   "   same
Son-Daughter none   "

F.P. and Photos Forward to: P.O. FBI TCP DPS

Place of Parents Birth. Father La.   Mother La.

Arresting Officers Boydson-Freeman   Division TCP

Charge or Crime Purse Snatching & Burg.

Modus Operandi and Accomplices Ludie Lynch

Disposition

.0.   Prisoner's Signature Johnnie Avie

Processed By Saragoza

New Photo and Description: Date   Age   Height   Weight   Right Thumb Print
                            Date   Age   Height   Weight
                            Date   Age   Height   Weight

Marks, Scars sc centered forehead; Sc lt arm;
Tattoos, Teeth none
Peculiarities lt handed; 9th grade in school;

IDENTIFICATION BUREAU
POLICE DEPARTMENT
TEXAS CITY, TEXAS

The following is a transcript of the record, including the most recently reported data and arrests, as shown in the Identification Bureau, Police Dept. Texas City, Texas, concerning our number:

8 8 1 1

FBI No.
DPS No.
FPC: 6 1 A2a 6
     1 tA2a

Johnnie (nmn) AVIE
M/M - DOB 8/20/1952

Date	Arr. No.	Officers	Charge	Case No.	Disposition
7/5/67	44053	Boydson-Freeman	Burg; purse snatching & Inv.Thefts (2 burgs, 5 thfts)	A-31461	Rel.to parents & J/O
3/5/68	45555	Eden	Theft & Inv.Burg.	A-34390	Rel.to J/O & Parents
3/9/68	45583	Steele	Dist. Peace	A-34460	Trans. Co. Jail
112/68	46993	Eden	Inv.Robbery by Assault	A-37731	Rel.to father 11/6/68 to see Juv.Off.Green
4/4/69	47880	Gross	Dist.Peace	A-39846	$25.00 fine, Rel.
7/29 '69	48577	Eden	Inv.Aslt.& Robbery	A-41341	Rel.to see J/O Green
1/24/70	49719	Scott	Intox. & Curfew Viol.	A-43802	Rel. $40.00 Fine
2/20/70	49884	Cohan	Simp. Aslt. & Shplt.	A-44139	Rel. $750.00 J.P. Bond
4-3-70	50319	Eden	Gaming	A-45077	Rel. $75.00 Fine
-21-70	50494	Ball	Indecent Exposure	A-45457	Rel. $25.00 Fine
-12-70	50845	Eden	Disorderly Conduct	No Report	Rel. $15.00 Fine
4-7-70	51224	Fleming	Intoxication	A-47213	Rel. $25.00 Fine
9/11/70	51241	Gross-Lawrence	Consu. Alcohol at Athaletic Contest	A-47260	Rel. to pay $75.00

IDENTIFICATION & RECORDS
RELEASE

Articles __1 LADIES GOLD TRIM WRIST WATCH__

__1 GOLD WEDDING BAND__

__PROPERTY OF MRS IDA C. DAVISON W/F 76 (DECEASED)__

__9-19-70__

Reason for Release _To Granddaughter Carolyn_

Inventory 9-22-76 4:31 PM

Released by, Auth. _B. J. DeWeet_

Released to _____ Date _____ Time _____

Returned by _____ Date _____ Time _____

Signature of Person Recd. _____

WILSON E. SPEIR
Acting Director

Commission
CLIFTON W. CASSIDY, JR.
Chairman
J. C. LOONEY
MARION T. KEY

TEXAS DEPARTMENT OF PUBLIC SAFETY
6808 N. LAMAR BLVD.
BOX 4087, NORTH AUSTIN STATION
AUSTIN 78751

Headquarters, Region 2
Drawer D Oak Forest Station
Houston, Texas 77018
October 6, 1970

Chief Rankin L. DeWalt
928-5th Avenue North
Texas City, Texas 77590

Dear Sir:

On September 21, 1970 you personally submitted the following
evidence: A house coat, slip, underpants, hairnet, pubic hair,
head hair, a wet blood sample, a vaginal smear, fingernail clippings,
and blood scrapings all from the victim. You also submitted from
the subject a shirt, pair of pants, pair of boxer shorts, a pair
of sandels, pubic hair, and head hair. From the crime scene you
submitted hair samples, teeth from the victim, grass found on the
kitchen floor, and a sample of grass from the yard.

You requested that we make comparisons and analyses to determine
the suspects involvement in this crime.

We have made our examination and wish to report that the blood
sample taken from the victim at the hospital was of type O origin,
that human blood stains were found on the shirt, pair of pants, and
shorts of the suspect, and that no blood stains were found on the
suspect's sandels. None of the stains were suitable for typing
procedures. We would like to report also that human blood stains
were found on the house coat, slip, under pants, and fingernail
clippings of the victim. The crusts from the right hand of the victim
were also human blood stains. None of the stains from the victim
were suitable for typing procedures. The blood on the sheet from
the hospital was also unsuitable for typing procedures. We would
also like to report that none of the hair found at the scene showed
any similarity to either the head hair or the pubic hair samples
taken from the suspect. The grass found on the kitchen floor was
molded and not suitable for a valid comparison to the grass taken
from the yard.

Due to contamination by blood the vaginal smear was not suitable for seminal stain determination.

We will retain the evidence in our files until we hear from you of a final disposition.

Anytime we may be of service, please feel free to call.

Yours very truly,

Major Jerry E. Miller
Commander, Region 2

By: *Dennis R. Ramsey*

Dennis R. Ramsey
Chemist & Toxicologist
Houston, Region 2

DRR:sr

cc: Galveston Co., DA

Other Books by Matthew Daniels Include

Suicide Note

Thicker Than Water

Big Game Hunting

My Beautiful and Loving Wife

Morning Motivation with Matthew Daniels Volume 1

Morning Motivation with Matthew Daniels Volume 2

Morning Motivation with Matthew Daniels Volume 3

Morning Motivation with Matthew Daniels Volume 4

Morning Motivation with Matthew Daniels Volume 5

Morning Motivation with Matthew Daniels Volume 6

Morning Motivation with Matthew Daniels Volume 7

Morning Motivation with Matthew Daniels Volume 8

Morning Motivation with Matthew Daniels Volume 9

Morning Motivation with Matthew Daniels Volume 10

Morning Motivation with Matthew Daniels Volume 11

Morning Motivation with Matthew Daniels Volume 12

All Available on Amazon.

Follow Me On Facebook:
Matthew Daniels

Follow Me On TikTok:
@matthewdaniels720

Made in the USA
Coppell, TX
03 July 2025

51471824R00154